THE BLESSED, THE DAMNED AND THE DEAD

A Collection of Dark Poetry, Twisted Lyrics, a Short Story and Eccentric Philosophy

Dominic R. Daniels

ISBN: 0692340939
ISBN 13: 9780692340936

Dedicated

to

Bruce A. Tiger

SLAUGHTER HOUSE NIGHTS

*M*achine gun hack, monster attack, werewolf nightmare. Time to slay, it's time to lay lambs to the slaughter. I'm the demon of night and the king of fright; it's time to kill the lame, welcome to the kill, to annihilations max. Whoa! Bring it to the altar; no one falters just to kill the weak at the Slaughter House Tonight. Slaughter House Nights.

You're such lovely freaks of desire. I'll set you free by my flare of fire. Feel the heat of the kill burn the flesh and feed your hunger with a meal. Deadly fun that can be shared; I will hear your deadly screams of fear. It's all fun tonight as you scream with bloody fear; set torches high; let them burn; eat the fire and let you burn with fear. It's a banquet of death, a feast of souls, delicious today. I set you free with deadly whims; unleash your hunger with cooked flesh of the dead. It's a slaughter that I desire, chainsaw death, laying down the law as the living scream in torture and fall. No law, no justice to call. Fuck you, the puny and the meek, time to kill the kids tonight, boil in blood that's right. It's slaughtering time to die for, I want to kill, I want to eat, time to thrill, time to scream at the Slaughter House Tonight, Slaughter House Nights.

Can't you hear the water boiling, children squalling, cooked meat, juicy feet, look there's a limb right there now we've gone too far, holy shit let's kill some more, Ha Ha Ha!

Could it be reason for fear or were our souls not there, but I am giving the sacrifice some spice, Umm eat the dead, evil fed, another portion please. It's all a massacre for murder time at the slaughter tonight. Lay the lambs to the evil to be fed, now I want to lose my head, the goats will rise for the ends time. Let the kings of the earth rise as we pillage and burn, so fuck the world. Slaughter and fight at the Slaughter House Tonight. Slaughter House Nights.

The demons call me; I want to be sold, killing time is near, feed me your fear, feed me your fear, Run now, run children bloody scared; I'll steal your souls tonight, a feast to give to the beast, as my dark master's pride is my reward. Laying lambs to the kill called murder at the slaughter. It's killing time at the Slaughter House Tonight. Slaughter House Nights.

Machine gun hack, monster attack, werewolf nightmare. Time to slay, it's time to lay lambs to the slaughter. I am demon of night and the king of fright; it's time to kill the lame, welcome to the kill to annihilations max. Whoa! Bring it to the altar, where no one falters just to kill the weak at the Slaughter House Tonight. Slaughter House Nights.

You're such lovely freaks of desire; I'll set you free by my flare of fire. Feel the heat of the kill; burn the flesh and feed your hunger with a meal. Deadly fun that can be shared, I will hear your deadly screams of fear. It's all fun tonight as you scream with bloody fear, set torches high, let them burn, eat the fire and let you burn with fear. It's a banquet of death, a feast of souls, delicious today; I set you free with deadly whims, unleash your hunger with cooked flesh of the dead. It's a slaughter that I desire, chainsaw death, laying down the law as the living scream in torture and fall. No law no justice to call. Fuck you puny and the meek; time to kill the kids' tonight, boil in blood that's right. It's slaughtering time to die for, I want to kill, I want to eat, time to thrill, time to scream at the

Slaughter House Tonight, Slaughter House Nights.

It's a sight to see; the devil laughs at me, so I spit in his face. I will rise. I am fear, ancient god of the fire. See me or hear me, I have you in the fire; now jump in barbed wire. Rat tat tat just like a bat out of hell's grasp; grab your gun and shoot to fire. Burn the feast, cooked so sweet; now feed my hunger, feed my shame, now I laugh at you, and you're a corrupted child from Hell's mass. I will feed your hunger and turn you to pain. Dance in death, Dance in blades; you're corrupted by fate. Suffocate your woman, tie the bitch up, now you feel the poison like a viper, feel the bite of the unholy snake. It's all the madness like spiders. Kill the world at the Slaughter House Tonight. Slaughter House Nights.

We're not going to halt now; let's go to Slaughter!!!!!!! Yeah!

UNLEASH THE BEAST

*D*on't say a thing. Hush your mouth. Bogeyman. Demon hands, the beast is near.

Devil man with black hoofs, dancing wild in the dust, make the kill; the time is right, slash the people; it's time to slay; what would your mother say? I don't know. I don't care. Time to be the serial killer; I like to strike some fear. Unleash the beast, the bogeyman is here.

Burning blades rings of burning fire, acid bath; kill the cat; shoot the shotgun, and make your move to play 'cause a killer's on the loose today. I'm out of my mind; you look so good to eat, and I am not too wrong, 'cause I got this hunger burning inside. I like to feed on flesh; I like you to bleed my children, so bleed good for me; you make my demons look good. Where is the beer? Now I got to drink 'til five. Hang you on the noose; break your neck with the fear hanging on. Tell me how you like your fear, medium burnt crispy or hell fire well done. Unleash the beast tonight.

Wrapped in deadly ways, I am trapped by the evil mime; dream the night-mare; make a scream tonight. Satan is the man that gave me demon blades; he who struck terror in me with fear. Slashers of fame, my heroes are the bogeyman; let's dance on the graves tonight. Razor blade claws. Machete mad men. Mini Gun rhythms blast the bastards with no care with no rhythm. Time to go to hunt and capture the kill; got a lot to do before the reaper calls my time, because I got to keep moving on. Unleash the Beast tonight.

Don't say a thing; shut your mouth, bogeyman. Demon hands, the beast is near.
Devil man with black hoofs, dancing wild in the dust; make the kill the time is right;
slash the people; it's time to slay. What would you mother say? I don't know I don't care;
time to be the serial killer; I like to strike some fear. Unleash the beast the bogeyman is here.

Baby we could not burn higher as I lay down my sacrifice on the pyre; now, devil doll, burn for me. Looks so fucking fine, as I feel the evil of the devil's fucking grip; keep telling you to cry for the weak. I don't think I'm on heaven's side but he is on yours, No, I was Judas by last week. Swing those hips, breaking whips. Scars and bloodshed marked massacre your worries. I take your fears. Kill the children; bring on the war. Unleash the demons; let the angels weep by Val Halla's flames--immortal blood, shining armor eternal fun--time to make the kill; the seeds of evil are more than one. Powers of the grave, the evil comes to feed as I take this battle axe and swing it in your face; full of blood with fear I piss on your grave. Free the beast; break these chains; I am hungry for death; I am hungry for war. Unleash the beast; the bogeyman is here; now let me taste your putrid fucking fear. Ha Ha Ha Ha.

Don't say a thing; shut your mouth, bogeyman. Demon hands, the beast is near.
Devil man with black hoofs, dancing wild in the dust; make the kill; the time is right;
slash the people it's time to slay, what would you mother say? I don't know. I don't care.
Time to be the serial killer; I like to strike some fear. Unleash the beast the bogeyman is here.

Baby, please don't be mad, join in the fun; hell you made me a bogeyman just like your daddy's one. Broken horns, bleeding wings, fallen angels from hell—now you sing on the devils harps you play for me. Could not be the way, but it is for me; I am damned soul to bleed; come on God; don't cry for me; I like being a lost soul now, I am going to burn and be free. Evil's living and heaven's dying to kill the light in me. Maybe I should have been a priest. No, I say kill the fucking weak.

Don't say a thing; shut your mouth, bogeyman. Demon hands, the beast is near.
Devil man with black hoofs, dancing wild in the dust, make the kill; the time is right;
slash the people; it's time to slay; what would you mother say? I don't know; I don't care;
time to be the serial killer; I like to strike some fear. Unleash the beast; the bogeyman is here.

Astral Plane. Demon gaze. Succubus with She Demon thighs. Hypnotic dreams deadly lies. Time to run and hide from the judge's wrath of Heaven's hammer strength. Madness fueling inside today, run hands stained red, running on the loose, hang on the noose, there's a killer ready to be fried.

Electric chair, eternal darkness fear, sin seemed never so sweet. Born to evil, born to slay, born to kill the weak today. Beastie ears and black heart ways. Unleash the beast in me.

Unleash the Beast. Unleash the Beast. Unleash the Beast—the bogeyman is here tonight.

SHE'S A THRILLER SHE'S A KILLER

*H*ey baby girl look at me; I tell you what I like to see: *lipstick lips, lace dressed thighs, lovely green eyes that sparkle and shine.*

You got it; I want it, to make your dreams come true tonight. You're a thriller dressed to kill.

Yeah you know it's time. Machine gun canons sound off for the queen of rock's life. She's a Thriller She's a Killer.

Motorcycle leather black, she rebel attack, born to dance on the cherubs wings of fire.

Straight to hoot, ready to shoot, make the kill for me this time. I want your body. I want your hate.

I want your love I want your fate. Join me now to the fight. Fuck the Man! Fuck the Law! It's free loving time. She's a Thriller She's a Killer.

Stand up for your right to rocks call. Stand up for your name. Stand up for the hour; now you're in charge of the game. Can you feel the power my love; rock with me tonight; take this stage my lovely mage; unleash your seductive spell on us all; I worship you like a goddess rocking strong.

Lighting fall from heaven's waterfalls. Sic em, yeah she tricked them with her lovely eyes that call. Spells of love. Spells of fun that make lovers freak and run. She's a Thriller She's a Killer.

I look at her; see such a sight, golden hair, scent is sweet, perfumed body that makes me freak.

Knee and worship her, goddess of the night, sexy wings of batty lovely bold, her fangs are sharp; she'll make you scream; her skin is cold. Hell kat honey I like to make that bet; be the bride of the night; be the bride of the night; for me, oh yeah. You're a thriller you're a killer that don't like to be told what to do to the Man! She's a Thriller She's a Killer. Strike to kill before sunrise.

Hey baby girl look at me; I tell you what I like to see:
lipstick lips, lace dressed thighs, green eyes that sparkle and shine.

You got it; I want it, to make your dreams come true tonight. You're a thriller dressed to kill.

Yeah you know it's time. Machine gun canons sound off for the queen of rock's life. She's a Thriller She's a Killer.

Shape shifting, pistol whipping, don't mess with the babe of the night, dagger in your black, now you're dead in the sack don't mess with that girl of mine. She's a Thriller She's Killer. Thriller she's a cold blooded killer; she strike you dead with her deadly eyes; the kiss of death is just fine.

She's a Thriller She's a Killer, She's a Thriller She's a Killer Keep rocking on this sea siren's cry.

She's wicked, sweet vicious, take a bite baby out of me anytime. She's a Killer She's a Thriller She's a Killer. She'll bathe in blood, bathe in mud or she's evil hot like the sun. She's a Killer She's a Thriller.

Hey baby girl look at me, I tell you what I like to see:
lipstick lips, lace dressed thighs, green eyes that sparkle and shine.
    You got it; I want it, to make your dreams come true tonight. You're a thriller dressed to kill.
    Yeah you know it's time. Machine gun canons sound off for the queen of rock's life. She's a Thriller She's a Killer.
    Make the kill or be killed today!!

MAKING SEX FUN AND LOUD

*H*ell baby doll, won't you come with me; let's go wild and have an orgy.

Sick and twisted but you know its fine, your giving those nasty eyes, Come on lets rock and roll while I dance to your lover's thrall; hold on baby I got to take this call;

Come on baby you want me strong; hold on baby we'll make it last long.

Gonna have fun tonight while we screw all night long. Hell yeah kiss me with those lips, damn you're like lighting you make me flip. We're making sex fun and loud.

Emptiness is no use to bring me no old mood; all I need is your love tonight; say hello to lust I love you tonight. Say hello to love at first sight; I kill ya tonight. Kiss to kiss, thrill to fall, damn baby you make me shriek; take a love pill. Making Sex Fun and Loud.

Fuck me once, fuck me twice, damn that's good I say it's like twilight.

Burning hot in the passion of the devil's delight. Hot night, hot fun; light the fire, we'll burn in dark love. Wicked ways. Wicked sin. Just fucking say it's so and damn grin.

Sure shot take a drink and smoke a lot. Cherry bomb, hell blast you. Wink your eyes you hot kitty kat. Making Sex Fun and Loud.

Open your arms as I put on your finger that diamond ring, I want your love tonight. Stay with me. Stay with me. I won't let you go. Don't cry for us. I will never let you go; no you're not going to fall just be with me;, I'll do what I can to make you fall in love with me. I will protect you from all harm; I be your angel of heat. Making love be strong my love's for you; is all time. Make it on with me.

Hell baby doll won't you come with me. Let's go fucking wild and have an orgy.

Sick and twisted but you know its fine. your giving those nasty eyes, Come on lets rock and roll while I dance to your lover's thrall; hold on baby; I got to take this call

Come on baby you want me strong; hold on baby we'll make it last long.

Gonna have fun tonight while we screw all night long. Hell yeah kiss me with those lips; damn you're like lighting; you make me flip. We're making sex fun and loud.

Breaking the rules; cracking the walls as those hot babe angels are gasping at us all.

Yeah hot red head; damn your good in the bed; now baby girl dance with me to heaven.

Making our noise to be heard; let's bleed some ears; let's smoke some weed; hell we just might make the harpies scream.

Hell baby doll wont you come with me; let's go fucking wild and have an orgy.

Sick and twisted but you know it's fine; your giving those nasty eyes. Come on let's rock and roll while I dance to your lover's thrall; hold on baby I got to take this call;

Come on baby you want me strong; hold on baby we'll make it last long,

Gonna have fun tonight while we screw all night long. Hell yeah kiss me with those lips; damn you're like lighting; you make me flip. We're making sex fun and loud.'

Bride of the light, baby be the bride of lights sin; dance with me in the rain, when you're wicked when your love is found. Making Sex fun and Loud.

IT PAYS TO BE BAD

*C*oming *riding on the highway hot; I am looking to the skies burning with sin*

A beast in me is ready to roar; Shot gun in my hatch, terminate and kill the dream.

Be the outlaw bat, just like a devil man. Shoot to kill, now from barrel to let the bullets fly loose

'Cause it Pays to be Bad.'

Got no worries like the kind man, because mama raised me born to be bad.

I live for no one except me; steal to steal, ready to kill. I'm wild like an animal, like a cannibal.

I am free. Waging to make war on those who want to the fight with me.

Biker heaven, Demon Women, Hell's Angels I salute you tonight as I ride through the flames.

Through the blue night through chains covered in blood. Fugitive of the night, rider of the dawn, hell demon cat that can't get enough. 'Cause it Pays to be Bad

Swing the bat; swing the axe, cut up the snakes, drinking blood, my rules, my ways.

Born to be bad just like the son of Sam, Go to the race with devils might as the ghoulies race with me on dragon wheels of steel today, race the race on hells plain. 'Cause it Pays to be Bad.

Fear the dark, fear the night I as I scream the grave ghouls light; feed the dogs; feed the hounds as Hells mouth yells out loud. Demon folk today come play with me, nothing is sacred today. Judas was my name; my God was not there when I fell by noose; now in Hell I burn; reborn to be resurrected by hell fire alive; born to race in flames dripping with sweat the biker from hell. Hell's emissary of death. I like to be free 'Cause it Pays to be Bad.

Got no worries like the kind man, because mama raised me born to be bad.

I live for no one except me; steal to steal, ready to kill. I'm wild like animal, like a cannibal.

I am free. Waging to make war on those who want to fight with me.

Biker heaven, Demon Women, Hell's Angels I salute you tonight as I ride through the flames.

Through blue night through chains covered in blood. Fugitive of the night, rider of the dawn, hell demon cat that can't get enough.

'Cause it Pays to be Bad.

I got nothing to fear, I was never saved but that's okay like I feel today; the flames feel hot like the dark demon power that flows through my veins, hell fire servant of eternal pain. Chosen to ride for the devil's pride that hell sent to steal, the lost souls of the damned today. Born to race; born to be free; I am sure that God is crying for me, but this I've heard that nothing matters to me, so why should I care what God wonders for me. Evil rules the night and hides by day light. Run with the night and fly with the dead, hide from the light that tries to get in your head. Tell me how to devour the light; feed on the night just as my dark father broke his covenant with God's might. Tear down heavens trees; bring on the night; kill the right, left hand ways are just fine with me. No mercy to the weak, no life to live, I feel no eternal peace that's fine because I am dead.

'Cause it Pays to be Bad.

Got no worries like the kind man, because mama raised me born to be bad.

I live for no one except me; steal to steal, ready to kill. I'm wild like animal, like a cannibal.

I am free. Waging to make war on those who want to fight with me.

Biker heaven, Demon Women, Hell's Angels I salute you tonight as I ride through the flames.

Through blue night through chains covered in blood. Fugitive of the night, rider of the dawn, hell demon cat that can't get enough.

'Cause it Pays to be Bad.

DUAL PATHIC WAYS

*C*rossing to paths, dual pathic ways, I see into your heart today.
The sickness burns inside saying what do you yearn, or should I say now will you burn?

Trapped between sins of the flesh, do what I do now I do my best. I do my best.

Two roads to take which one you will choose will be your fate. Dual Pathic Ways calling to be heard Dual Pathic Ways calling me; which do I turn. Traveling down dual paths of time, one life, one death. one soul for all time.

What is the one will you choose when you've got all to lose, which is the cure for your hurts and wounds.

Which is the heart you follow or hers to keep, what say will you by whose God to seek?

Trapped and lost in time, I heard of what my heart lies to me to be heard. One answer I have to say is why try at all when the dark I seek I want to *fall. Dual Pathic Ways calling to be heard Dual Pathic Ways calling me; which way do I turn?*

Seeking the answers of a broken soul, when one can say there's a devil in us all; yet the light of God lives within us all an angel of mercy to whom do I call. God help us;, how do you say like angels that were cast out now cry and bawl, now cry and bawl, now cry and bawl. Two roads to take; it is choosing time of what eternal waits at the end of the line. Now at the final seat, it's judgment time of the final reap for all mankind. Dual Pathic Ways calling me which do I turn? Two forces call me what do I yearn?

No calling to be left alone; they want to be heard; Heaven and Hell's voice must be learned.

   Poor weeping angels call for me; I cry for you; such fools you were when God cast you out to the earth. Now you die and now you cry; now you die and now you cry. All damned immortal foolish fools.

What is the one you choose when you've got all to lose; which is the cure for your hurts?

   Which is the heart you follow or hers to keep, what say will you by whose God to seek?

Trapped and lost in time, I heard of what my heart lies to me to be heard. One answer I have to say is why try at all when the dark I seek I want to fall. Dual Pathic Ways calling to be heard Dual Pathic Ways calling me; which way do I turn?

Now you see the reason; there's a lesson to learn of why you can't be forced to serve who you serve; two choices to take, nothing else to learn. This is all there is; we are trapped on God's green earth. Now I say to you, who will you serve as you see a man trapped between the edges, who just might burn.

Dual Pathic Ways, call to us of all; two choices to take; which one will you follow to make by your call. Human ways, Human ways, Human ways. I live for only today. I want to escape from this call of the pawns God made of us all. I will set you free with music's call, so come with me and set your-selves free from the call. Oh come with me, come with me away from it all.

What is the one you choose when you've got all to lose, which is the cure for your hurts?

Which is the heart you follow or hers to keep, what say will you by whose God to seek?

Trapped and lost in time, I heard of what my heart lies to me to be heard. One answer I have to say is why try at all when the dark I seek I want to fall. Dual Pathic Ways calling to be heard Dual Pathic Ways calling me; which way do I turn?

Now you see the reason; there's a lesson to learn of why you can't be forced to serve who you serve, two choices to take nothing else to learn. This is all there is; we are trapped on God's green earth. Now I say to you who will you serve as you a man trapped between the edges, who just might burn. Dual Pathic Ways, Dual Pathic Ways, Dual Pathic Ways!!!!!!!!

DOWN AT THE ROCK SHOP (BABY TONIGHT)

Soon as the sun goes down
the street lights begin to shine
looking for a party to go to.
gonna rock the city tonight
So grab your girl and your buddies too;
show this town who's the rocker in you.
Rock on Down at the Rock Shop Baby tonight.

It's a party town, a party town so shock rock it tonight.
Time to mosh, time to roll, time to howl in the pit below.
Blazing wheels screeching sweet hellfire delight. Out late
drinking, no deep thinking, having one hell of a time.
Sweet honeys, green money; fuck the law; it's chaos time.
Raise some hell at the show tonight,
Bad girls, Bad boys rule the scene till dawn's fair light.
Sweet rocking sweet mocking at the Rock Shop Baby Tonight.

Thrash your guitar; feel the power of the hour let you through.
Roll your joint; let the weed set the mood.
Blasting brothers, crying mothers, don't have nothing to say to you.
Rebellion flying, hot timing, gonna rule the world at first sight. Hell's
Rocking shock rock Baby tonight.

Ignite the sky with fire to burn with light. Rock and Roll ain't gonna die.
You're the band, you're the stars, you're the crew, you're my family of rock-
ers too.
Snake poison, blood flowing in my veins so true, sweet death I kiss you with
delight.
Wild women get mixing, let's get it on Down at the Rock Shop Baby Tonight.

Canons blasting, girls flashing; hell you're in heaven by nine.
Drunk lucky, storms thundering, party on into eternal night.
My sweet children, the dark father's willing to free you with rock's might.
Down at the Rock Shop Baby Tonight.

Fallen raining, no shame, you're a freak and you ain't no angel.
Set the time, the pact is made, the evil's here to give you fame.
The dark watchers are my followers. Come on down here and play with me.
Mad killing, blood filling, adrenaline building at this party tonight.
Keep rocking; keep shocking Down at the Rock Shop Baby Tonight. Yeah!

DON'T WANNA GROW OLD
I WANNA DIE YOUNG

Don't wanna grow old; I wanna die young.
Don't wanna grow old; I wanna die young.
Hell baby girl come play with me and make desire.
Sing like those burning lips are filled with red fire.
Blue eyes, sexy thighs, make those legs swing like a smokin' ride.
I want you to love me, I want you to hug me, I want you hold me in your arms.

Party all night, smoke all day, drugs, sex, and booze the only way. Party hard. Party hot, oh now you want to play.
Be rocking be talking about those hot babes I want to say. Keep moshing keep rocking about midnight I got to play.
Don't waiting; I am not hating; sorry honey but I got to go my ways. I don't know where to go but I know I want to be free

Rocking on the wraith's deadly wings. Hell I want to fly; Hell I want to glide; Hell I want to never grow old for my mortal life.
Immortal love, immortal fun, drink from me you will set you free. Take control of the flow as your eternal kiss enthralls me.

Don't wanna grow old; I wanna die young.
Don't wanna grow old; I wanna die young.
Hell baby girl come play with me and make desire
Sing like those burning lips are filled with fire.
Blue eyes, sexy thighs, make those legs swing like a smoking ride.
I want you to love me, I want you to hug me, I want you hold me in your arms.

I am your slave; pour the blood on the fire; let it burn, let me bleed; cut me up and let me scream.
Give me torture; give me pain. I am your blood servant of Hell today. I see your weeping eyes, oh mistress, love why do you cry,
Oh, why do you cry, don't you want me to die? No I don't want to be old; I want to die young, Steal the night, steal my sight, hold me tight, let be in eternal dreams this night.
I crave your love; I want your blood; make me your deadly fiend. See my eyes glow; can't you feel the heat. Sexy blight deadly sight, suck my blood tonight.
Because I
Don't wanna grow old; I wanna die young.
Don't wanna grow old; I wanna die young.

Tainted blood, tainted fun, oh you make my heart burn with evil love.
Give your money for the run now, so keep sucking, don't be mocking, baby now don't fuck with me.

I want you baby to want me. Rouse Red in the bed; bury your fangs in to my neck and feed. Superstition in life; don't stop your strife.
Immortal love, immortal fun, oh I love to be bad; it's better than mortal love. Don't stop now; kill my soul this night, Send my soul to eternal sleep; there for your return I will wait for you to keep.
I love you now forever night my mistress of night.
Don't wanna grow old; I wanna die young.
Don't wanna grow old; I wanna die young.

Kill or be killed that is the law. I want your evil thralls; take me or hate me, or turn me into your vampire lover delight.
Taste my whim, rich deep sin, let's burn hot tonight. Dancing in the flames of death. Rock and Roll rocking on dragon fire tonight.
Breathe me deep, now steal my heart to keep, let me sleep among the bones under the walls. Corpse to freak, the angels weep, I want to die young baby.
I love you now forever night my mistress of night.

Don't wanna grow old; I wanna die young.
Don't wanna grow old; I wanna die young.

DEVIL IN DISGUISE

*H*er kisses are hot just like mine; her lips are so soft sweet divine; her love is so deep, she makes my heart bleed inside; I wait for her at the graveyard by midnight. Taste the blood, taste the blood, taste the blood of vampiric life. Walking undead she's looking fine, walking bluish pale in the moon light. Run blood red, now your body's undead as you feel the call of the night.

I love the feeling of this fight; taste the hunt to kill your victim's life. Drink her deep like rich red wine. I taste her soul just like the Lord's bride. Walking and waiting in the night, she's a devil in disguise.

Come on honey baby make me feel alive; time to go hunt and feed like a parasite. Time to take it to new deadly heights. Take me now to the light; I'll give you a crown of Lucifer's light, fallen weeping angel baby I weep for you tonight. You take my spirit away and now you scream; I drink your love till you cry for me; I want you so baby I will protect you my lovely she demon of darkness's glee. She's a devil in disguise.

Come on my bride of darkness, Come on baby scream, Come on my darkly girl; kill the weak with me. Let's have some fun to slaughter come let's just be freaks, time to take out meek.

Come and let's play in the underworld for some fun, techno beats thrilling to kill; seek out your hunger and enjoy your meal; feed on the power of guns; shoot to shoot; let the bullets cut through to flesh of some. Psycho killer, mass murderer, evil deed's done; feed your vengeance tonight. Just like she walks, like those lips talk, she's a devil in disguise.

Glory to her I will give, her I worship, my deadly sin. You I miss the girl of my past life.

Missing your wish, missing your kiss, now you're just a dream no more; I want to see you but I am not sure. Red hair, blue eyes, such a hot lover you were; you were my life. Now, you're gone for now I will see your vampire eyes in this fantasy of mine. She's a devil in disguise

Her kisses are hot just like mine. Her lips are so soft, sweet divine. Her love is so deep she makes my heart bleed inside; I wait for her at the graveyard by midnight. Taste the blood, taste the blood, taste the blood of vampiric life. Walking undead she's looking fine, walking bluish pale in the moon light. Run blood red, now your body's undead as you feel the call of the night.

I love the feeling of this fight; taste the hunt to kill your victim's life. Drink her deep like rich red wine. I taste her soul just like the Lord's bride. Walking and waiting in the night. She's a devil in disguise.

Love's talking to me to call you soon; your sweet love made me feel alive, I miss you baby now.

So I cry. Now, back into the mortal world I am down, looking into the blue of the night, Such a sadness sinks inside to see you gone; I miss your love tonight. You were always good to me; now I will never have you; your gone because of me. Your hot love burned inside but now you're gone the love of my life. You were like the flames, my she devil in succulent heat. She's a devil in disguise.

Her kisses are hot just like mine; her lips are so soft sweet divine; her love is so deep; she makes my heart bleed inside; I wait for her at the graveyard by midnight. Taste the blood, taste the blood, and taste the blood of vampiric life. Walking undead she's looking fine; walking bluish pale in the moon light. Run blood red, now your body's undead as you feel the call of the night.

I love the feeling of this fight, taste the hunt to kill your victim's life. Drink her deep like rich red wine. I taste her soul just like the Lord's bride. Walking and waiting in the night. She's a devil in disguise.

DEAD ALIVE

You can run but you cannot hide;
look around you're dead inside.
Feed on his flesh of life.
Dead Alive, Dead Alive, Dead Alive.

The zombie nation marches with you, feeding on your mother's children
too.
Fucking, killing, sweetly thrilling, massacring the womb; torture is near to
feed the fear
as the living dead come alive. Dead Alive, Dead Alive, Dead Alive

Boom stick time, chainsaw will, let's kill some living dead; it's time.
Animals bleeding, women screaming, the sacrifice is ready to be destroyed.
Necro fed, demon heads, as the fire burns to rise, possession is one tenth of
the law, seeking to destroy who
let you fall. Conjure the spell, the incantation's made, let the evil fill the
night.

Torn to shreds, bloody heads, as the angels of death call, the headless horse-
man rides from the wood holding the heads
of deceased hoods. Time to feast on the bloody feast of terror; come with me
my friends come and fear.
Dead Alive, Dead Alive, Dead Alive.

Batty bitches, sexy witches, big tits that make me feel fine; let the night-
mares come to life.
Grave robbing, monster clobbering; the beast comes tonight. Satan's laugh-
ing, hot she devils licking my blood just right;
let's party tonight.

You can run but you cannot hide;
look around you're dead inside.
Feed on his flesh of life.
Dead Alive, Dead Alive, Dead Alive.

Come on give me pain, come on give me paradise, pain, pleasure, paradise.
Pain, pleasure, paradise,
Pain, pleasure, paradise

Cut the flesh and eat it right; cannibals devour the light, evil's sweet oh red
meat, look at her; its slaughtering time.
Slice to slice, dice to dice, kill the lambs and taste the soul's sight.
Come on power of darkness; come on power of hate, set the power of the
night, party in the bone yard late.
Dead Alive, Dead Alive, Dead Alive.

You can run but you cannot hide;
look around you're dead inside.

Feed on his flesh of life.
Dead Alive, Dead Alive, Dead Alive.

Ancient warriors rise from the grave, seeking to slay as they call.
Bloody battlements of armor, rusted steel, make my unholy fall, rocking
zombies with guitar thrilling.
Hear the voice of your masters' call, worship the night, kill the light, join
in the party with us all.
Slaves of death, no sin will rest, indulge in your hunger's law, magic blast-
ing, spirits flying, madness raving,
Let the ghoulies destroy the walls. Embrace your destiny, let it be the law.

You can run but you cannot hide;
Look around you're dead inside,
Feed on his flesh of life.

Dead Alive, Dead Alive, Dead Alive.

CIRCUS OF FREAKS

Die for none and ready to go, let's rock this show and make Hell explode.

Die for none and behold the dead rocks in the graveyard below; so make yourself known to terror, your nightmares are coming to scare, be prepared for your end is near.

The freaks of the night are here, to terrify, to chill your bones; they'll make your blood run dead cold. We're ready to raise hell for some fun; if you don't want to die, you'd better run.

We're a Circus of Freaks and we're coming to get you.
We're a Circus of Freaks and we want to play.
Be dead. Be wild. Oh, misbehave.

We love to party with the dead all night and day; we play electric guitars with vengeance and hate. We're maniacs with chains on our backs, necks detached, stitches on our faces, our skulls are showing, bones and cracks, our minds exploding, we're full of pain, full of rage, it's just inhumane.

The freaks of the night are almost here, to terrify, to chill your bones; they'll make your blood run dead cold. We're ready to raise hell for some fun; if you don't want to die you'd better run.

We're a Circus of Freaks and we're coming to get you.
We're a Circus of Freaks and we want to play.
Be dead. Be wild. Oh, misbehave.

Fear the main instinct; don't like it kiss our feet; we're on the beat, hungry for you, sick and insane; we like to be known, don't want to die; you better run home to mommy and daddy who don't know; light the fires, it's time to scream and moan.

We love to party with the dead all night and day, we play electric guitars with vengeance and hate. We're maniacs with chains on our backs, necks detached, stitches on our faces, our skulls are show-ing, bones and cracks, our minds exploding, we're full of pain, full of rage, it's just inhumane.

With us it's Halloween every day; we'll walk the earth for a thousand years; earth will hear us with it's bleeding ears; no time to stop, not time to think, just be afraid and you'll never blink. We're ready to raise hell for some fun, if you don't want to die, you better run.

We're a Circus of Freaks and we're coming to get you.
We're a Circus of Freaks and we want to play.
Be dead. Be wild. Oh, misbehave.

We're on the beat, hungry for you, sick and insane, who likes to be known; you don't want to die, you'd better run home to your mommy and daddy who don't know; light the fires it's time to scream and moan.

You'll never survive the monster's rage; be prepared to die in your grave. We're just Circus of Freaks. we're coming to get you and we want to play. Coming to get you and we want to play. coming to get you and we want to play. HA HA HA HA!

CRAVE YOU

I need you, I want you, I love you, I crave you!!!!

I see your luscious lips, your sexy eyes; you make my soul burn inside.

I find myself wheatear away, the pain grows day by day, trapped inside this world of shame, makes my heart bleed when you're away. All I know is I miss you every day; I'll die for you then lose you anyway. I crave you tonight.

Feast the kiss of sweet lover's bliss as your evil blood flows in my veins, salt sweet death, your forbidden kiss, the kiss of death is the game. Lovers die. Lovers bleed. I dream of you in torturous screams.

Destroy the evil in which the world holds, make us dream of destiny we can mold; find yourself; feel alive; I'll set your soul free by fire's path; your heart full of darkness, come with me and float in dreams, fly away in clouds of fantasy. I see light, I see day, I see night, the stars are bright, truth in verse. I am peace, I am hope, I am the rope, please don't die, don't give up on hope, I love you so, please don't go, don't leave me now, please don't go. 'Til death do us part you're in my heart, 'til the end of days. I crave you tonight.

Feast the kiss of sweet lover's bliss as your evil blood flows in my veins, salt sweet death, your forbidden kiss, the kiss of death is the game. Lovers die. Lovers bleed. I dream of you in torturous screams.

I need you, I want you, I love you, I crave you!!!!
 I see your luscious lips, your sexy eyes; you make my soul burn inside.

I find myself wheatear away, the pain grows day by day, trapped inside this world of shame, makes my heart bleed when you're away. All I know is I miss you every day; I'll die for you then lose you anyway. I crave you tonight.

I need you, I want you, I love you, I crave you!!!!
 I see your luscious lips, your sexy eyes; you make my soul burn inside.
 I find myself wheatear away, the pain grows day by day, trapped inside this world of shame, makes my heart bleed when you're away. All I know is I miss you every day; I'll die for you then lose you anyway. I crave you tonight.

You gave me a new way to live; taught me to be someone instead, time to live or time to die, look into yourself; please do try; you have pride; don't let that die; please be mine. We'll rock the world, we'll party all day, peace be inside, because I crave you, I crave you, I crave you tonight.

DOOM BUGGY
(BURN BABY BURN)

In the depths of the underworld below, the challenger awaits me, gonna find out if he's going to show, make no mistake I won't let this race be blown; rage in me is going to show; let revenge be known, time has come; the race has begun; all bets are closed. Let my doom buggy run the show, do it Doom Buggy Burn Baby Burn, do it Doom Buggy Burn Baby Burn, Burn Baby Burn for me.

Blazing my wheels through the fires of hell, dead man come to mock me, let it be known I'm in control; no one's gonna stop me. Racing from the devil's wrath, living out my own path, no fear in me, I love to ride on the wild side, nothing can stop me. Do Doom Buggy Burn Baby Burn, Do it Doom Buggy Burn Baby Burn, Burn Baby Burn for me.

God's speed be with me tonight; time to fight the good fight, adrenaline, heavens speed is the vice in me, no fear I have, courage in thee, destroy evil and the world will be free. Do it Doom Buggy Burn Baby Burn, Do it Doom Buggy Burn Baby Burn, Burn Baby Burn for me.

Let vengeance be known; the time has come; the race has begun; all bets are closed, going to let my doom buggy run the show; lost souls everywhere; the reapers of death come for me; they'll not win, God's angels are with me; nothing can get in my way, no one's going to stop me. Destroy the devil, Satan is dust, I kicked his ass in the bust. Do it Doom Buggy Burn Baby Burn, Do it Doom Buggy Burn Baby Burn, Burn Baby Burn for me.

Destroy the darkness, destroy the mean, kill the cruel, let goodness be seen.

Coming down the end of the line, making my mind to live, evil must die, evil must go. I will make hell explode, temptation tries to screw my mind, but God believe in my time, I made history; the world's watching; the time is mine; victory made down the line, down to finish do we dash first in place, evil's defeated this time, justice shines upon me. Oh Yeah!! Do it Doom Buggy Burn Baby Burn, Do it Doom Buggy Burn Baby Burn, Burn Baby Burn for me. Yeah!!!!!!!!!!!!!!!!!!!

EMBRACE THE NIGHT

When I look up to the night
I see the power of the mages light
Calling me up but I want to go down.
I feel no pain in being found, no need to fear.
Come with me children of light. Come with me and
Embrace the Night.

Eternal Life, Eternal Love, Mortality is a joke just like mud.

Darkness comes, darkness goes, be careful now or I'll consume your soul. If you
don't see the power, then you'll never know, the vampire curse is upon you now.
Accept your fate and fight now. Embrace the Dark, Embrace the Night,
Embrace the blood of undead life. Accept your fate and fight now.

Eternal Life, Eternal Love, Mortality is a joke just like mud.

Don't be scared my child tonight, come with me and embrace the night; the
power you have is now in you; never die, never grow old, you'll never fall
into the unknown; accept what you are or you'll never grow.

Eternal Life, Eternal Love, Mortality is a joke just like mud.

In the world of blight, we kill by no code of right, live in rage, bathe in blood, enter my world where magic appears; night by night, you become fear, hunger grows; fuel the bloodlust within your soul, sing your fangs into flesh; you can bet it's better than sex, come with me children of light, come with me now and Embrace the Night.

Eternal Life, Eternal Love, Mortality is a joke just like mud.

Forget humanity, it's pointless to want; take the gift, destiny's come, believe in your immortality, dark vibes, romance burns; I will protect you my children; you're my blood, darkness comes, darkness goes, what's the future, I don't care, I don't know; fires burns in the heart's wake; the spirit of freedom will you take, you're above the world's tears; can you feel the strife? feel the life? feel the fun? come with me, you are the one.

Embrace your right, your rebirth delight, come with me and Embrace the Night.

Eternal Life, Eternal Love, Mortality is a joke just like mud.

When I look up to the night
I see the power of the mages light.
Calling me up but I want to go down.
I feel no pain in being found, no need to fear
Come with me children of light Come with me and Embrace the Night.

LITTLE MISS WITCH

Hey little miss witch you sexy cat, you put a spell on me and that's a fact.

You got black magic and furry cats, your fangs are sharp as vampire bats.

Hex to Hex, Vex to Vex, Kill to Kill, the Spell is right. Succubus, you're my wife.

You love to tempt me with your enchanting eyes; let's make love with hell inside, never let me go; I want to feel the pain of being tamed, turn on me and you'll be slain. Never die with long goodbyes feel the heat inside.

Hex to Hex, Vex to Vex, Kill to Kill, the Spell is right. Succubus, you're my wife.

Hey little miss witch you sexy cat, you put a spell on me and that's a fact. You got black magic and furry cats, your fangs are sharp as vampire bats.

Hex to Hex, Vex to Vex, Kill to Kill, the Spell is right. Succubus, you're my wife.

Cauldron of darkness, drain the light, look into my eyes and you'll be mine; can't you feel the blurring inside. Magic, water, fire, blood; make my heart burn with sinful love. Hear the thunder, feed your hunger, feel the lust of sexual heat; indulge your heart to your fantasies beat, turn your body and dance for me; let me take you on a trip, to the darkest dream, crack the whip.

Hex to Hex, Vex to Vex, Kill to Kill, the Spell is right. Succubus, you're my wife.

Time for your darkness to face my own light, who will win the fight of fights, who cares about life; you taste like fire, my old flame of desire, your blood is cold just like mine; I feel free and so do you, don't be ashamed we're not through.

Hex to Hex, Vex to Vex, Kill to Kill, the Spell is right. Succubus, you're my wife.

Little miss witch you sexy cat, go put your spell on me, you won that's a fact, entrap me, I love that, I drink your blood and make you scream, feel the lust of my ecstasy. My lady of night come to me and be my queen of fright, I'm your creature of the night, do this thing for me, I'll be your slave you gothic queen!

GET THE GROOVE ON

*H*ear the sounds of the room as you listen to the power of music's tunes, hang with your love and begin to play. Get the Groove On with a kiss, having fun at the club; you cannot miss. Get the Groove on you can make your move, when the music flows, it will help express your love so, express the power of your soul this way.

When true love flows I go, to pledge my heart to her. Eternal love that can never be taken away.

Sweets to the sweet and love be to your beloved as you dance to the soul of moon light's embrace, lovely bliss, while you're drinking champagne, Dom Perignon with your babe, feeling just love sweet innocence could not be so bold, as I hold her with tenderness in my arms. Get the Groove on get it on today, Lovers will make love in passions heat; no time to be sad to have the blues. Get on the Groove and prove your true love to her heart to her today.

When true love flows I go, to pledge my heart to her. Eternal love that can never be taken away.

I always tell her the truth, to flirt or to play let your inner hunger tell you to set the mood as you show how to dance on the stage. Embrace the beast as you dance wild to your lover's heart beat, show out the crowd that you're the stars today; you can feel the lighting strike the room as you rise like waves in the seas of the people's ways, just like you know you want to do, just prove what you have to do, hear the power play. Get on the Groove and see the colors of red rouse as a lover's kiss blossoms and blooms. Get on the Groove this way, you're the angel and devil dancing on the stage as you tempt her soul with romance today.

When true love flows, I go, to pledge my heart to her. Eternal love that can never be taken away.

So tender a moment I wish it would never go away, while feel her lips lock with mine in this eternal game of the afterlife. It's true, an angel and devils kiss to be a few, I pledge to my angel my love to be so true, no one shall part us not even the few, eternally made, twin souls, twin flames to dance to forbidden loves woos, to masters I see, were just two slaves who serve the other side of each two, how strong will our love last during this strange feud. I know today that we'll run away and escape the eternal blues of war and pain; all I see is rage, it deep down breaks my heart to say. So dance with me for forbidden love to the mood, where two souls can choose to be in love with who they choose. Get the Groove On; get it on today, never fear we'll be safe and run away, let it rain I'm in no pain as long as you're with me my angel rouse, a tender sweet kiss unite our love and be so true.

When true love flows I go, to pledge my heart to her. Eternal love that can never be taken away.

Unmasked and not betrayed, in this masquerade let our love be strong, as we try to go and right which is wrong. Get the Groove on today, don't stop loving you in anyway, my eternal love is true. I cannot stop thinking about you. When true love flows I go, to pledge my heart to her. Get the groove on and set the mood. Get the groove on and set the mood. Get the grove on and set the mood.

WRAP ME IN DARKNESS

*F*alling into the past, falling into old dreams, I am looking all the way down; will I fall because of you. Why do you make me believe I still have love for you? Upon my dreams it seems, that nightmares are really true. O why, can the pain you gave to me I now give to you, O why do I feel escape is gone to down the tube, the way to the lights is through, Darkness in sleep comes to shield my soul, my sorrow I unleash on you. Wrap me in Darkness O how I cry for you.

The memories I can't let go that make me think of you, the past is filled with pain inside, I can't find the light today, my world is broken it's true. Upon time I think to myself, the world has paid its dues, in darkness and dreams I am free from the past of you, so wrap me in Darkness of how I cry for you.

When you see Hell inside, you will know Hell too; the life I led is now dead, I am through; O why the Hell does the past come into view, the love once shared has died consecrated into glue. Time to learn the truth, I want to see beyond the stars to see a world away from you. Time to dream away. I cry out unto the darkness, let me become one with you. Eternal dreams.

Eternal Sleep. Let the past be through. The sadness feels it will never die. life is dead for me. it is dead for you. So wrap me in Darkness, O, how I cry for you.

Can't begin to say the anger that I feel for you, Regret and Grief is all I have for you that I once knew. O, why has society become so wrong the world is full of fools.

   Darkness Come to me now, shield me from the face of you, the past sears my soul, love dies and grows anew.

Wrap me in Darkness; Wrap me in chains; Wrap me in Heavens Arms I know how the world is dark for me, it's dark for you.

BURN IT DOWN,
BURN IT BLACK

*B*urn *it down, burn it fast. I see you smile at Hades, fire by death, fire by pain on your finger. I can't stand to see all you crying babies. Screw the past and its meaning, it pointless at all. Forget your pain and burn your mercy to music's call, Rock on darkness take your anger and burn it out to the call.*

Burn down Burn it Black the Banshees are giving me a call, death by spirits, ghost and ghoulies, fires my call, destruction and violence are burning my way to the fall, Come on!

Sadness and Sorrow, forgotten mourning like the omens of the crow's caw, ghoulish spirit, deadly wishes of love, I spread to you all, forget your shit, pain and worries, just rock on, Burn it with fire, burn it anger, let your rage be your law.

Why live in misery in past at all, the future is bright and that's what I like, I think I'll take that way today. Dreams and Goals is what you need and Love above all, Red heads, Brunettes, leggy Blondes are the girls I'll call. Come On!

Burn Down Burn it Black, Halloween is the Fall, Darkly wishes, dreaming desires I wish to you all.

Passionate fueling the lustful burning of the flesh in us all, learn the thrill of the bloody chill, when your beast howl's and balls, let the fire grow fast higher, as you dance to your lover's thrall, see meadows through the corrupter's window of your soul's wall, you can't escape to flames of fire while you burn to the call.

Burn it Down, Burn it Black to seduction's call, play with fire burn your finger, let your rage be your call, break it down, bring it black to dreaming desires law, bring forth the flame, power by fire, of red hot desire, now say fuck the pain.

Sweet loving sirens, not letting me crying while they take me far away, love is hot, love is burning, to the fame, power and glory, let not love be mourning. Fuck the devil in every way.

Playing guitar, rip string flooring, rock the hell away, listen to metal, now let's party today, burn down burn black, let's fly away, dream on higher, to heavenly desires to set us free today, burn it down burn it black rock on today.

BAPTISM BY BLOOD

*B*ring me blood running red to the altar's call, as the Lord God commands to all, slaughter to praise, power to cleanse, the sacrifice of the Son of Men. Blood for blood, tears for tears to wash away your lies. Time to live for the fight to survive so come on in bathe, bathe in the spring of the sun, bathe in holy blood, Master of light, Lord of right, this is the one, rocking hardcore to the son in charge of heaven's skies, baptism by blood.

Could you understand the waters that fall from the light, my blood to fill your weeping souls that are mine, my life now to be with you, come with me to kill the Devil tonight. I will never forsake you now let's go to fight.

Servants of God, Servants of Yah come forth to join the army of the king of kings might. Be our avengers of the holy light. Let me avenge your law tonight, fly with me to city of the Father, to destroy to defy, to fucking kill the devil getting inside. If I can be a power man let me be a rocker of God this day and night. Rock on Christ, who gives you his power to save you from the fire, blood of Christ, body of life, time to bathe in his testament. It's the blood the sacred blood that saves, come to me my children and live, bathe in my life for you I gave. By my grace you will born again, born again, come on!

Sharpen your swords for the days of war have begun; hell it's revelation time has come; let's have some fun; open your wings of armor and fly from your pit; your new archangels to be my warriors fit, kill with holy fire the devil's pigs are near. 'Tis time the dogs of hell are here; be ready to strike the wicked today, what bloody hell is pain. Anti Christ has got nothing on me tonight.

Could you understand the waters that fall from the light, my blood to fill your weeping souls that are mine, my life now to be with you, come with me to kill the Devil goals tonight. I will never forsake you now let's go to fight.

Baptism by blood, transform into the light, warriors of mercy I guide you all, come to the pool of angels I call, come in live, live in the new heaven life. Virtue blessed by righteous deeds, you will become immortal just like me;, JC is the nick name; let's kick some demon ass today.

Could you understand the waters that fall from the light, my blood to fill your weeping souls that are mine, my life now to be with you, come with me to kill the Devil goals tonight. I will never forsake you now let's go to fight.

Screw the bitches; I am for heavens kisses, as my lady angel of love watches over me all the way. Time to go to throw the devil's head into the fire, praise the light, praise the light let's go and fight! Everybody Rock and roll tonight, Rock to God, Rock the Christ, Rock my friends to the children of the light! Baptism by water, Baptism by fight, Baptism by right, bathe in the blood of life, the kids are knocking on heavens doors tonight, Baptism by light, such a sight, such a strike,

Baptism by Blood

LOOKING DOWN THE PERISCOPE

*L*ooking down, down in the darkest deepest night, I see she is there standing such a sight, I think I want to call her, to tell her how much I think of her, that she is really real. Say to myself that she is the one I've been searching for; there's none other I rather be with or, all I can think about is you. Yay! Yay! Yay! You drive crazy about you.

Looking down the Periscope of life is what I dream, do what you want to do, I tell you what it means, to be happy just being you. Looking down Periscope I see you all today, I think I am feeling funny now to be with you, you make my heart melt, when I am with you. Kisses past sunshine love, hugs past the glee, I think of what I was looking for and now I know it's you.

Yay! Yay! Yay! I'll walk one day to her door, putting the ring on her hand, making her my bride and walking on the sand, holding tight than ever before, Can't begin to think what love is for, Because I got it bad, All I think is her. Yay! Yay! Yay!

Since the Day we first met, I thank God for that bet, things have been going on, walking down past the stream, all we can think of is our dreams,

I look at her and tell her I adore that darling love she shows to feel, Happy and Glad than ever before who thought young love could be reborn, Yay, Yay, Yay.

Looking down the Periscope she is all what I need, swimming along together like fish in the sea; I want to let her know that she will always be mine; I'll keep her in my heart and never let her go. Why does it seem to me, when I lost hope in love, you came to me, baby, baby.

Looking down the Periscope, saying to myself she's been the one I've been searching for. Yea Yes, she is my armoire, now and forever more.

THE BETRAYER

*"The betrayer comes; he makes his way; he slays
the innocent, his words are pain; the betrayer
pretends to be your friend; he takes away from you,
and makes you sin."*

*The betrayer! The betrayer! The betrayer comes; he's
a thief in the night, he's willing to steal your
life; the betrayer comes, the betrayer comes, he's
ready to come and strike, the betrayer comes, the
betrayer comes, he wants kill your mind, the
betrayer comes, the betrayer comes, he would take
away your wife.*

*The betrayer thinks he's your friend in the day,
you think he's your friend but he's really fake; he
wants to take away your pride, steals your visions,
steals your time, he makes you think he's your only
friend, he's a false deceitful, son of a bitch, he*

*steals behind your back, he cheats you every time,
he tells terrible shit all the time.*

*The betrayer must die, the betrayer must pay; it
will cost his life in vengeance name; the betrayer
will die, the betrayer will pay, vengeance is
furry, vengeance my name.*

*As I came home in my sleep, I found an innocent
bloody sheep, my wife and child were vile, turned
to stone by the Devil's child; the betrayer was my
friend, I thought him to be, he committed the
ultimate sin; betrayed my family, stole from my
pride, stole a piece of my soul, the betrayer will
fall tonight, die and fall.*

*The betrayer must die, the betrayer will pay,
vengeance is furry vengeance my name, the betrayer
must face the ultimate price, they lose a
friendship like losing a life, they will fight
inside, feel the pain of wails, I will laugh when
he is in Hell, Ha Ha Ha!*

*Maybe then the next time when the time has come,
there be no betraying on this good son, the
betrayers have been and will always be, evil men
have died in their own way gone, sons of Judas,
sons of Baal, when the fools are done they run they
flee, crying out loud in scary screams.*

*The betrayer must die, the betrayer will pay,
Vengeance is furry vengeance my name.*

THE HANGED MAN
RISES AGAIN

*T*hough *I wait in darkness, I lay in the depths of the threshold of death, the time has come for my resurrection to proclaim my name, to destroy them, filled by a code of honor within me, destroyed by who I trusted and loved, they hanged an innocent man in cold blood, killed my name, stole my life, my wife, my love away, that is their game. I paid the ultimate price, ready to make the most important decision of my undead life, the hanged man rises from the grave, steals the souls he loved to claim.*

The Hanged Man Rises Again

Lost in anger, hate in mind, thirst for blood, vengeance is now. I am justice, judge and jury, the verdict is mine, the guilty shall pay, I am dead and I will unleash pain, Hell fire in my soul today. I'll slay the ones who did this to me, make them suffer on the Hangman's Tree, every time I pass by the graves, I see the souls of the dead, those who like me were betrayed. I weep for them, but find them not, the call to me for justice, we've all been wronged, executed by tyrants and evil men who should be flogged, the good and innocent shall win this day, I am the Angel of Death, justice is my game, the hanged man rises from the grave.

The Hanged Man Rises Again

My eternal mission is to avenge all souls wronged, save the weak and kill the evil strong; bring God's wrath on all of them, I'm trapped inside this world of rage, disease, and plague, passing through the time of eternity, save the souls of damned, the goal of mine, revelation, redemption, salvation, this is my purpose, this is my cause, avenger of those who have all been wronged, later find escape, end the hatred in my chest, Free me O Seraphim, from my curse, let me rest in peace one day that I may sleep, in dreams of light and deepest love, no more killing, no more death undone, grant me endless rest, end the vengeance in my chest, let my heart explode with fire and water, blood on snow, blade in flesh and taste of death on my lips, to kill the ones I desire the slay, who strayed from the path of virtue many days long past today, the hanged man rises from the grave.

The Hanged Man Rises Again

Forever I walk in fog and mist, dancing sweetly in eternal darkness, dancing my bride of the damned, my lost soul wife who I would kill to bring back, and so I walked in the town, to tavern where bloody drunks and lusty wenches abound, filled with tears of wine and brew, did the shutter at the sight they saw, walking death did I grew, the devil face such is a man, I am the Demon the and Angel of Revenge. Look not for pity when I strike, I bear my fangs with venomous delight. They looked on me, the ones who killed me, they fainted on my satanic sight, my eyes of blame did I look and ate their souls out of their corpse flesh husks, drinking them deeply did I enjoy the taste of their sins such sweets tastes like sugar power bread. But there was one who had no fear, I extended my rotting claw to his brow, the was the one who caused my fall, I grabbed him tightly by the neck, I said to him, die this day, you evil fiend, prepare for judgment, for this I was raised, now for your shitty soul I will never pray, Die! Die! Die!

You're going to burn in hell, and I will laugh for I will haunt the world because of your evil craft; now you will be filled with terror, be filled with fright, for this day, you are forsaken by Heaven's sight, in weeping and suffering you will never see the light of day again. Scream, Scream to Life for It is now gone, I will be in your nightmares forever.

The Hanged Man Rises Again

Hung him thus by the noose, just like me did break his neck too, wriggled did he and wriggled he did, desperately trying to get free but he did not, I tore out his heart and ate his brains, so succulent such a death this was to be, I think I will continue to kill and avenge you and me. The Hanged Man Rises from the grave, steals the souls he came to claim.

The Hanged Man Rises Again

These were my thoughts, when I saw the evil in me. I am a killer and avenger. So I go and slay, avenge and kill, kill the whole evil world this day. The just I will let live, the wicked I will not, children shall be safe for I will not harm them, or their mothers who nurse them; no, only evil men shall die. Protect the innocent I shall do, I am an avenger of broken souls; I will show great mercy on the weak, but the wicked strong their souls I shall keep.

The doomed shall be my eternal slaves, until I decide their punishment is full and paid. I am a wondering soul in the night, never at peace, never at rest, a wandering harbinger of eternal death. I am destruction, I am fear, I stand tall and beyond strong, I do not forgive those, who spill innocent blood, their heads I will claim until my work has been appointed done.

The Hanged Man Rises Again

POWER TO POWER

*U*ntil the day comes, when heaven cries, till the forces of warriors reign from the sky, I will not be alone, not for you, not until the darkness takes me down, I don't know what to do. All I can do is be strong for a day and fight the fight every way. Until the time comes to death today. I will not suffice or give into you! This is the hour, this is renewed, until the judge comes I will be few, the power rises to be in view.

Hour to hour I wait for you, come to me now with my soul in tune, cant describe what he says to me, to take my heart away from God's heavenly tree, I can't take the pain that is to true, Your sin is my sin, Sinful mood. Blood falls flowing into Jung, I don't know what I will do until the time has come. Then I will be New. The soul of many men screams for you, O Lord Yahweh come to me now I need you, Power beyond Power I kneel to you.

Dark desires rise inside, while I feel the blood curdle inside, rage crashing thru the glass for you, I don't what to think Or where I have gone, I cannot think where I belong, I don't know what the truth says to me, faith decline from heaven's beams, Power to power the final hour to see the truth. Reveal the light please, I need you.

The gates rolling high, but I am losing the way to eternal life, O why do I act this way in the life I choose? I can't escape the sad song of life, why can't addictions fall out of the way, I don't want you, your sinful glow chains me to. I rather have died then to ever have met you.

Now He comes to claim the time is right, so I am fading fast I'm fading fast tonight.   Power to Power I pray to you.

WELCOME TO THE ZONE

Ba Bop Ba Ba Bop Ba Bop Ba

Set the time to play, you're ready to get in the game, see the screen blur light up all pretty and cool, time to settle the score, get even once more, so coin up and be ready to play, zone on into play, Welcome to the Zone.

Fight your right you're the pretty name, you're the dream master you're in the game, Cut cut down the baddies today, you always wonder why they were there anyway.

Ba Bop Ba Bop Ba Bop Ba

Level 10 here you roll, time to take on the boss and more, load up your gun and fire away, you ready be sharp to make a killing tonight, Boom boom bang bang bang, the bastard is dead this way.

Yeah!

Ba Bop Ba Bop Ba Bop Ba

Traveling back through the portal to world of mortals roam, we hope you've enjoyed your stay, you kicked ass today, so come back sometime soon, you will know where you want to go, come in and play, Welcome to the Zone.

Ba Bop Ba Bop Ba Bop Ba

Life is a game every day, play the way choose, just make sure you don't lose, because if you do then you say, there's a price in every choice you make, go into the world today, little warrior bring the world some pain, be strong, be brave, fight for justice in humanities name, now begin to play.

Ba Bop Ba Bop Ba Bop Ba

Puppets of the hour, Puppets of the age, Humanity's fate is chosen by a few of that we choose to say, Kings and Queens of the Realm, Corrupted by greed, evil ways, the people become the mindless fools, believing the things they are told to listen to, time to face reality, bring truth to your brains, learn to become vigilant and face the world, if you don't there be no freedom or hope for you.
   Ba Bop Ba Bop Ba Bop Ba
   Welcome to the Zone

THE DAY HAS COME

*T*he Day has Come, In the valley of Megiddo the war has begun, demons and angels falling to the scene, fighting ghastly to decide to end, men and women screaming in cries, they know it's time to die, the Holy One comes down descending from above, dressed in red robes and a golden crown, sword in hand, the Law is bound.

The fallen warriors rise from the dead, leading off to deceive men, fallen from grace, fallen by pride, The Watchers come fast like the sands of time. Stealing fast the souls of life, I feel I am falling for a time.

The bloodshed spreads across the land, here he comes the Son of Man, Cities crumble and nations destroyed, Fires fall from the sky burning down the sins of rhythm.

The Books are Open and its decision time, of what you did in your life, if you've lived your wicked life then you will burn for all time, It's such a sad thing to see, when all we had to do was obey Yah's authority.

I wish to think it's all a dream, but how Can you hide the past from sinful deeds, fallen from faith and lost in time the truth has been hidden exchanged for lies, man will do what he wants leaving corruption what he wroth, so I say declare your thoughts.

Make a choice of whom you serve, God or the Devil, to whom you turn. Fighting the fallen from all time, when you live in the darkness in half the life.

Standing at front of the Great white throne, awaiting Judgment to see your fate, burning in Hell for what you take.

The Day has Come, In the valley of Megiddo the war has begun, demons and angels falling to the scene, fighting ghastly to decide to end, men and women screaming in cries, they know it's time to die, the Holy One comes down descending from above, dressed in red robes and a golden crown, sword in hand, the Law is bound.

SEX MACHINE

Do you like it hard, do you like it fast?
  Do you want it slow; do you want it to last?
  I don't know what to say, because you're looking at me that sexy way,
you say baby I want some fun so come on here and show me some love. I got
to say I like this task, and I'm going make it forever last,
  Sex Machine.

The lights go dim, the music flows, the candle light begins to glow, we begin
to kiss, passion explodes, the heat is rising, no tears for crying, the craving
rises with ecstasy, so let me show you how the magic flows, you say never let
me go, you Sex Machine, Oh Yeah! Wedding Night Tonight!

Hot and heavy your very fast, take off your shirt and let's dance, just come
on and give it to me love, You're a wild girl but I love you like that, we're sex
freaks and we like it like that, were just a couple of Sex Machines, Oh Yeah!

Dancing in the moonlight I feel the power of sexual love explode, I crave
your love, your mind, your body so, the device of life, your heart grows,

you set my soul to bleed the blood of fire, you are the one I desire. Wedding Night Tonight!

The beasts in us begins to show, I am losing control, the carnal desire has been exposed. Let's burn in passion, let's burn in love, or we can just call it good ole fun. Do you feel it baby, because I sure do Ha Ha Ha, Were Sex Machines.

Bridal love, tough love, hot love, give it to me now, let's rock right now. You're my wife for life! Creatures of the earth, Creatures of the dawn, just like an explosive bomb, Ha, Ha, Ha. Sex Machine, Just a couple of sex machines. Wedding Night Tonight!

Do you like it hard, do you like it fast?
    Do you want it slow; do you want it to last?
    I don't know what to say, because you're looking at me that sexy way, you say baby I want some fun so come on here and show me some love. I got to say I like this task, and I'm going make it forever last
    Sex Machine, Yeah.

POOLS OF BLOOD

*R*ed stains hit the floor, I wake up feeling numb, I see my hands cov-
ered in blood, what is happening, what have I done, could it be that
the deed is done, I find myself standing in Pools of Blood.

*I can't believe what I see, is it really real or am I just dreaming now like
I should to feel, I can't begin to fear what I may have done, could it be a
victim more than one. I want to escape but I can't run, everywhere I turn
I see my soul laughing at me when I am none. Could it be that the deed is
done, I find myself standing in Pools of Blood.*

*Here I see the shadows come, I can't begin to think what I have become,
The dark world cries for me and that it always does, but how can you cry
when you have tears for none, a million children calling to me, a million
sorrowful cries, Could it be that hunger that I know I hide inside, Because
right now I see myself I see myself standing in Pools of Blood.*

Red stains hit the floor, I wake up feeling numb, I see my hands covered in blood, what is happing, what have I done, could it be that the deed is done, I find myself standing in Pools of Blood.

I feel so weak that reality's not real, I feel myself falling away into the dark realm, or could it be not what I think thought, I'm running to the body that lies here and here above, I can't believe what I see can it be only true, I am undone, destroyed and dead, and saved by none. Blades stuck in me, my body bleeding badly, this is who I was, who killed the innocence of youth, when sadness fell into view, Trying to remember who killed me, who was the one. For now I find myself standing in Pools of Blood.

Fuzzy and fading out life, Until what is that what I see now falling into anew, a picture I'm holding of him, I see his face and I can't believe its true, but I guess the price you pay when you have friends like I do. Bleeding and Betrayed the circle now unmask the clues, I see myself falling, falling truth, could I see myself what I have gotten into. The deed has been done, I am a ghost just like you, daddy was right when he told me to be careful about the friends you choose.

A tortured, tortured man, a lost soul, what can it be that the evil in me is also in you, Don't have nowhere to go or really should, my spirit weeping now feeling none, Because I see myself, I see myself standing in Pools Of Blood.

NIGHTMARE RIDER

*T*he skies are getting darker, air has gotten colder, rustling from the wind comes the scent of death, rain starts falling, rivers of blood flowing, as the rider in black comes to me. Dark and tall dressed to kill the reaper comes in glee. Rider from Hell, rider of sin, I see your shadow inside me . . . Nightmare Rider.

Caped in Scarlet blood, killing time has begun, the rider comes to claim the souls of the dead, he makes his demons crawl in pools of scum, scythe in hand and ready to strike like a devil man, hunter of souls, hunter of grim, how do you shine, Nightmare Rider.

The graves rattle in shame as the reaper passes by, in pursuit of man how do you come to kill our kind, hunger of blood, hunger of pain, the slaughter is thane, a face is seen of evil eyes, how do you know the pain of life, you see the sins of mine, time to kill and time to die, a sadness twist the mind, why do you come to take away all that is mine . . . Oh Oh Oh Nightmare Rider.

I see your claws, bones and all ready to rip the flesh of mine, I am facing you now and I know your mind, I know its my time, Going to see the blood of life my eyes are blind, Magic of blight, mage of whim, I am ready to die . . . Nightmare Rider.

The skies are getting darker, air has gotten colder, rustling from the wind comes the scent of death, rain starts falling, rivers of blood flowing, as the rider in black comes to me. Dark and tall dressed to kill the reaper comes in glee. Rider from Hell, rider of sin, I see your shadow inside me . . . Nightmare Rider.

Nightmare Rider O why do you haunt me, why do you haunt me, why do you haunt me. The time is now, I am clinging to the flesh inside, darkness coming, I see a cloudy line, slipping away from this world, to the other side. Slipping away and falling down to the final time.

Laying down to the rest till the end, bloodlines severed from time, judgment will come to claim us all, the angel of death was mine.
Nightmare Rider.

LIGHT IN THE DARK

Fog, Wind, Air, Night, Time to live or Die, Time to Live or Die, Beauty is past the mysterious things I see, past the darkest night; I dream I see, Stars so bright, this is the Light.

Light . . . above. Light . . . above, Light in the Dark Night, Wonder and delight is passion of life, can you see the world past in what you seek when you find the meaning of the dream, Light!

Marvel, Love, Faith, Life is the greatest thrill of all; Life is a Mystery to all. When can you see the future, I Cannot tell, but Hope is a way, the Light I see, Its Light, Hope, Wonder, Enchantment so, Imaginative a world beyond your Own.

Heaven, Hell, Light, Dark, Reality past the mind can hold, dream of the place you want to be, walking through the city of Eternal Gleam . . . There is Light, There is Rhythm where music is the soul the songs of time.

Light in the Dark Night is What you see, Can you behold its secret mystery, Light out there shining bright, I see your face filled with sight, and you just might have found paradise tonight, Light!

Fog, Wind, Air, Night, Time to Live Or Die, Time to Live Or Die, Beauty is past the mysterious things I see, past the darkest night, I dream I see, Stars so Bright, this is Light.

Come into the Light, Child Of the Night; Come into the Light, Child of the Night . . . Light in the Dark.

HEAVEN'S SO FAR AWAY

*U*pon the day I have fallen from grace, I find myself controlled by fate, I am living day by day, blind and fearful and fueled with shame, addictions from the past haunt me now, they never pass, I'm a sinner again not a saint, I feel nothing but anger and hate, I am such a fool today, I cry to God to give me strength but I all I hear is a silent phase, Heaven's So Far Away.

Lovers lost and friendships destroyed, how I retreat in vice, pain is my sacrifice, blood into tears and tears into stone, O how my heart has become so cold. I'm floating far away. The saints of Heaven are calling to me, but I can't lift my tired wings, I find myself falling into Hell, Heaven's So Far Away.

Lust and greed has become my sin, O how I hate it now and then, when will my vices come to an end, sadness suicide are yearning to burn, but the Father tells me this is not the way, sadness has grown into pain, Heaven's So Far Away.

What do you do when your off the ropes, when you have lost it all and have no hope, what will I do today. I am not free, free will is such a lie to me, Evil hearts and evil ways, May God help me in my Shame. Where do you go when you have nowhere to turn to, when your world is gone, until your firm, Heaven's So Far Away.

O Holy, Holy Christ forgive please for my blight, I am weeping hard for the bread of life, but what do you do to kill your shame, prayer helps but addictions are pain when your addicted to sinful games, how I hate who I have become, I am lost from goodness into shame, Heaven's So Far Away.

Is there hope for a sinful world, is there peace for bloodshed seen, is there love when love is gone, is freedom there when your down on your luck, is there Heaven in the stars above, is there goodness when addictions come, how do you fight the evil of one, I do not know what to do, for now I am angry and full of shame, Heaven's So Far Away.

FORBIDDEN DREAMS / (FORBIDDEN LOVE)

*W*hen *I first met you, I thought you're the one that could be, when we first kissed it seemed heavenly, now you're gone and I am all alone, but it's rebel time indeed, I'm happy that you're gone, Blood stain kisses were a distant thing, a sadden theme that took me down the way of the path of darkness realizing the darkly desires of my evil deeds, in the deepest darkest night of my forsaken dreams.*

Sexy sweet demoness eyes I see, such a sweet desire of evil love that you unleash the werewolf in me, Time to go into the night and hunt among the moon lit howling green, I feel that you could make me kill these shadowy passions in me. Such a crippling sight to see that you took away my breath bringing my very soul to the deadly sin of Forsaken dreams.

Beautiful butterfly burning blood, make my heart tingle like you know you should, sexy queen of darkness, my lost girlfriend of gothic love. You'll always be inside my secret woman when I close my eyes, my deadly forbidden bride in my sweet sensual memories.

Now I find a whole new world of fright in the journey of life, Time to face the demons I call fear inside my mind. Time to ride into the night, on my darkest raven hair black stead sweet midnight, searching for the true love of my desire, now is the time when I release the beast in me.

Howling with fangs drawn and claws sharp and bleak, I feel my fur grow as it creeps on me, time to find my prey to have a bloody sweet evil feast, of freshly love, of fresh blood, make the demons run with fear as I make them burnt crispy done. Time to run, time to climb; time to seek adventure in the moon pale light. Yet in my sad little howling I will still remember the love we shared that is when I we see you at night when I close my eyes to sleep, you will always be in deepest darkest forsaken dreams.

Beautiful butterfly burning blood, make my heart tingle like you know you should, sexy queen of darkness, my lostly girlfriend of gothic love. You'll always be inside my secret woman when I close my eyes, my deadly forbidden bride in my sweet sensual memories.

Where is the one, I want fun, to have little lady wolf running along with me, to the pines, through the night, through the deepest darkest windy part of my mind, O it's time, to go for the chase, love is just a race, to find that one true sweet lovely lady I will spend the rest of my life, You know it's time, you know it's right. Yet looking back into the past I still miss that girl that took my heart away in that old rhythm, passions fueling my heart still with the signs of pain, such a tender embrace of darkly fantastic gothic fun I call forbidden love.

Ripping off the flesh of my scared soul, I feel the monster inside begin to ascend, take me into the world of myth and forgotten lore, where bizarre and insanely nightmares can run and roam inside my sick twisted mind, time to make a story to tell, Love was Hell, as her sinful sweet lips close with mine. Beginning to let out the inner hunger from my life.

Beautiful butterfly burning blood, make my heart tingle like you know you should, sexy queen of darkness, my lost girlfriend of gothic love. You'll always be inside my secret woman when I close my eyes, my deadly forbidden bride in my sweet sensual memories.

Now I pray to God, set me free O set me free, set me free from this hellish twisty lie, a serpentine babe who was the love of my life. But the sadness comes into the scene, like playing back a bad home movie, happiness comes and goes, breathes and bleeds, yet still inside when I close my eyes I will see her lost, my little lovely vampire girl in my forsaken dreams.

FIRE UP THE NIGHT

*D*own, down in the darkest night, He calls to me from the land of fright, under graves, under the bones, beyond the Styx of the abyss in bold. He welcomes me with an evil smile, come on down here to the dragons den, if you do then you're damned dead.

Fire up the Night, set the torches to burn, see the flames rise and lost souls churn, hear the cries of the evil ones, who lost the hearts of golden sons, devils laughing humanity cries, dark deception, darkest lies, here is my corpse that I lay for all time. You're damned dead.

Burn, Burn, Burn, dance around the fire, chaos rules the night, see the tables turn, I am the tragic hero, can't you see my broken wings shine, I am the foolish angel of light.

Fire up the Night, the mystic age swarms, let your nightmares come alive, see the madness inside, The time has come to set to destroy, the fireballs will rain from the sky, trapping the realms of men for all time, You're damned dead.

Tortures come from all the sides, killing me all the time, red hot pokers, burning chains of steel, the time is right, the time to kill, Burn down the world, the fire pits alive, madmen screaming I'm possessed in my mind. You're damned dead.

Burn, Burn, Burn, dance around the fire, chaos rules the night, blood raining down falling to the streets, the heretics laying entombed burning in the city of Dis.

Down, down in the darkest night, He calls to me from the land of fright, under graves, under the bones, beyond the Styx of the abyss in bold. He welcomes me with an evil smile, come on down here the dragons den, if you do then you're damned dead.

FIRE!!!!!!!!

ALL DOWN HILL

*A*ll the people crying, innocent teenagers dying, being killed in the street, what is going on in the world today, life is hell in every way, I can't find the truth to say because it's not here today, what good is left in a cruel world this day. It's All Down Hill for you and me.

Violence and bloodshed spreading along the way, what is the reason for dying, to see families pains, I don't know what to say, time for a change, will the world see a new day, I think not we're all going to the end in a sad game.

Someone out there is thrilling to seek a bloody killing, the agonizing death of the lame, evil seems to be winning, the devil must be grinning, to humanities rage, what are people thinking, what are the things their speaking, to feel the wrath of vengeance today, all the good must suffer why evil laughs in sulfur, they will find their end along the way. It's All Down Hill Today.

What the Hell is wrong with people these days, they don't give a damn or the same, I can't stand to see such pain, the world might deserve just to burn, when there is no goodness in a world to learn, there is just one thing that has to be said, I hope good men learn the truth before they're dead.

It's All Down Hill for this day, The angels are crying, many people dying, where are the heroes to save the day, They seem to be missing or crying in shame, only lost souls feel the pain. Justice needs to be trying to fake its name, justice is a lie, why do the innocent have to pay.

Violence and bloodshed spreading along the way, what is the reason for dying, to see families pains, I don't know what to say, time for a change, will the world see a new day, I think not we're all going to the end in pain, turn to Jesus, together let's pray, sacrifice in prayer will save the day.

All the people crying, innocent teenagers dying, being killed in the street, what is going on in the world today, life is hell in every way, I can't find the truth to say because it's not here today, what good is left in a cruel world this day. It's All Down Hill for you and me.

DEAR LITTLE ANGEL

*D*ear angel little angel how far we have gone, long its been since last
we spoke along, the hardest thing I did was leaving you, I wish
I rather die than to see you go into the blue. But fuck the tears fuck the
shame. It's time to get my shit together and go play.

Cut your heart out and make it show, praise to play to the gods of rock
and roll.

Angel love, Angel love, remember the first kiss we shared. Miss you so,
I miss you so, yet my heart is not there, got a feeling to go, got a will to be
free, got a desire to let my rock flow! Detroit! Detroit! Detroit Motor City!

I am alone too just like you I still miss you but I'm not to sad I think of you
when I can but don't be crying my Angel Love because in my heart you'll
always make me glad, your hot love helped me believe in you and hope is
there too. True Love and Sex are always a hot hell high like snorting blow.
Mosh out Mosh in step back hear the thunder explode!

Time to go to Motor City Sweet Rock and Roll.

Angel love, Angel love, remember the first kiss we shared. Miss you so, I miss you so, yet my heart is not there, got a feeling to go, got a will to be free, got a desire to let my rock flow! Detroit! Detroit! Detroit Motor City!

Dear little angel, don't hate me so, I got to go far far away, until the pain in my heart goes away, time to take the doctors call, that's where I be, Rocking Detroit baby. Shock the Rock! Kill the Bong, smoking my mad momma's ganja!

It is when that time arrives that I will see you again and our old friendship can be reborn to beat the blues. Hope your rocking strong too.

Angel love, Angel love, remember the first kiss we shared. Miss you so, I miss you so, yet my heart is not there, got a feeling to go, got a will to be free, got a desire to let my rock flow! Detroit! Detroit! Detroit Motor City!

Do not be sad that I am gone, for it is not for long but understand that I will always love you in my heart even when you have found someone new, one day I will see you soon remember always the love we once shared, because that is where we will always be to. However I see the fun to addictions kicks, stings like a cobras kiss, hot damn, hot chick, you were a goddess to fuel. Until the time comes go I'll be rocking with my guitar buddies too, here in Motor City Sweet Rocking Rolling paying my dues.

In my Dreams I see you and it makes me feel alive so keep thinking of me and one day we will be rocking on stage to duel. I will see you in time, we are one heart, one spirit, one soul, come on all praise to play to the gods of rock and roll!

Angel love, Angel love, remember the first kiss we shared. Miss you so, I miss you so, yet my heart is not there, got a feeling to go, got a will to be free, got a desire to let my rock flow! Detroit! Detroit! Detroit Motor City!

Hold up your flames, we'll light the way because true love never dies and it never is truly gone. Going down to Motor City, Rock City, Sweet hot, Sweet spot, monster shocking lets rock and roll!

DOESN'T MATTER WHAT I SAY

*I*t doesn't matter what I say, it doesn't matter what I do, she does not love me anymore. I feel the pain when bitterness burns away. How will she be with me, I am lost insane inside, can you feel my devil inside. The shadows come to burn. I will die when I say, there is no return, and love is not the worth, to make me feel this way, Burn the world today.

Feel Hell inside you and will know the flame, Bring me a heart of coal my heart has grown cold, in darkness shields me now; I am hell in mourning pain. Can't describe these feelings that I feel, so why should I feel this way, for the girl I once knew, I will never be the same, rush me in a flame, set the fires to burn, love is not the worth, than to know sadness today, a broken heart's soul is nothing yet at all, they don't want to hear but I will make them pay, To steal their happy dreams away, come in my fire to burn, there's nothing I haven't learned, who cares today, the world is full of pain, in thus what you feel, it doesn't' matter what I say.

I don't give a damn what she said to me, she can kiss my ass for all I care, some girls never learn when the truth comes out, they sulk and cry and bitch it out, that's just fine to say goodbye, you were not the one for me, *now the world is new, and I am so ever free, love was such a joke, but I can see that my heart is dead, Hell I'd rather live in vices and sin.*

 It doesn't matter what I say, it doesn't matter what I do, she does not love me anymore. I feel the pain when bitterness burns away. How will she be with me, I am lost insane inside, can you feel my devil inside. The shadows come to burn. I will die when I say, there is no return, and love is not the worth, to make me feel this way, Burn the world today.

 So Rush me in a flame, set the fires to burn, love is not the worth, than to know sadness today, I will make them pay, To steal their happy dreams away, come in my fire to burn, there's nothing I haven't learned, who cares today, the world is full of pain, in thus what you feel, it doesn't' matter what I say.

DREAMING ALONG
THE SKY TONIGHT

*L*ooking down past the line of the day, feel my heart float away, it's hard to try to live each day when you live in the past of yesterday, can be feeling what my heart says to me, what is the future what is the dream, I find myself flying on high, looking to the stars for love by night, and when I hear the sounds that call to me it will be the day she comes to me. Oh I am Dreaming along the sky tonight.

Dreaming to find what dreams mean, can destiny be found when I am free, can't begin to tell the feelings that I feel, Oh I just can't stand to be away, from love of below and above, when will I find that darling love, I can't stand to be without her, to find the one that make me free, Love is what I dream, It's like candy taste so good to me, I taste her kiss and is so fine, taste like honey all the night, making love under the stars to the women I marry will be my wife, be my feeling ever free is what love is to her I see, A dreamy girl I see when I sleep, Oh Oh why can't you come to me.

Looking down past the line of the day, feel my heart float away, it's hard to try to live each day when you live in the past of yesterday, can be feeling what my heart says to me, what is the future what is the dream, I find myself flying on high looking to the stars for love by night, and when I hear the sounds that call to me it will be the day she comes to me. Oh I am Dreaming along the sky tonight.

When I think of her I know what she'll be, just a blossom darling from heavens trees, like flower of truth that never dies, oh oh how I cry, Can't describe this feelings that I feel tonight, Can't wait to see that dream girl tonight, oh oh my heart burns to feel the heat lovely passion what I see, Two lovers together and Free, Just sitting together under a tree, talking about things that lovers do, when will I find her is the dream. I know you're out there and I believe. Oh Oh Oh!

Looking down past the line of the day, feel my heart float away, it's hard to try to live each day when you live in the past of yesterday, can be feeling what my heart says to me, what is the future what is the dream, I find myself flying on high, looking to the stars for love by night, and when I hear the sounds that call to me it will be the day she comes to me. Oh I am Dreaming along the sky tonight.

When is the time that lovers meet when true love is blooming and it sweet,
    I keep my head on high, looking for the One all the time, I see you dear and I know you dream too, looking for the One just like me, Ooh why is love so hard to be when your Dreaming that it can be, can telling you darling what you'll mean to me.

Looking down past the line of the day, feel my heart float away, it's hard to try to live each day when you live in the past of yesterday, can be feeling what my heart says to me, what is the future what is the dream, I find my-self flying on high, looking to the stars for love by night, and when I hear the sounds that call to me it will be the day she comes to me. Oh I am Dreaming along the sky tonight.

FATE OR FURY

Fate or Fury, Furious Fire, Choose your Fate, Choose your Fire, Bring me a soul to cleanse this day, bring it to the Fire,
    Heavens Fire, Heavens Name, Get up here and face your trial.

The test has been laid out to you, you want to be free, you better choose, what's your poison that you desire,
    Show me a name to call your shame, Pitfall soul you should reek in pain,
    I know you're the stuck in the dark today.

Climb up the mountain to prove your worth, If you can't then you're a fool, fighting to live, fighting for faith in the Most High, your hanging on by a slender line, it's time to see if your worth the grade, you don't want to see my angry side, now climb or die.

Fate or Fury, Furious Fire, Choose your Fate, Choose your Fire, Bring me a soul to cleanse this day, bring it the Fire,
    Heavens Fire, Heavens Name, Get up here and face your trial.

Here is your sword I give to you, time face the evil in you, destroy your evil, destroy your hate, destroy your demons today, redemption time has arrived, if you want salvation then repent your crimes.

The devil is a crafty fool, wishing to kill all humans too, it does not matter who you are, Satan laughs at you. Kill the evil inside your soul, show me there is humanity left in you, bring me your anger, bring me your pain, kill all your addictions or die this day.

Fate or Fury, Furious Fire, Choose your Fate, Choose your Fire, Bring me a soul to cleanse this day, bring it the Fire,
    Heavens Fire, Heavens Name, Get up here and face your trial.

Is it Fate or is it Fury, That I leave up to you, In case you didn't know, I am the same as you. Fate or Fury, Fire and Shame, Let the Darkness burn away.

JOURNEY TO THE MOON

*L*ooking to the sky I feel the sun begin to lift I am looking on high holding my breath, Time has begun to surely spilt I'm ready to blast off and throw a fit, Time get moving and fly on high, I'm ready for the journey to go in my space ship. What can I say, IT'S TIME TO ROCK!

Are you ready to rock, are you ready to roll then if you can let your spirits go, set go set the course to take a trip, riding through the winds of the sands of time I am upon the ship, take the journey, Journey to moon.

Nebulas past the darkest skies, burning down the stars of time, night turns night for the days ahead, the coldest point beyond the dead, playing my guitar and free from men the darkness calls to me again.

Journey to the Moon, live past the dream, free the power of Rock to set you free, take the trip beyond what you knew and you will see something new, welcome to the party welcome to scene, because here in space you can be what you want to be.

The air gone and world is bleak from what you see beyond millions of feet, who gives a hell what you seek. Just here and look into your soul, your fantasies rip like you've never known. Rock to the beat, Feel past the mold, then you will be free beyond humanities hold.

Journey to the Moon, Rage in the Sea and thousand light years from where I want to be, so I'll set the course Where I want to be, a party out there just waiting for you and me, then I'll Know that I'll we'll free!

So Come with Me, to the moon if you're scared then you're a fool, can't seem to find the way, then I will let you know, I be your guide into the unknown, can't you see the light is calling for you, then you will know the space man in you.

Time to take a ride and never fall, when you feeling the best rush of all, time to take a chance to go beyond the scene, in space you'll never have to scream, Bring your fear to calling, and come with me.

If you can take the step then you will believe, will you take the Journey to moon, The Journey beyond what you have seen.

LIVING ON HIGH FOR YOU

*C*limbing up high, climbing up fast, I am on my way to you, Climbing up high, Climbing up Fast, I can't wait to hear the sound of your voice tonight, Climbing up high, Climbing up fast I am going on the journey to You, I am dreaming to fly in your arms tonight. Live it out loud, Live it fast, I Am Living on High For You!

Love that way she looks at me

Through the trees, through the stars, I'm thinking of you, Running through streams, swimming in ponds, I hear the love of you, I want to say I want to be a part of you, the love I need, the love I seek I see in you. Oh Oh Oh I am set free with you.

Love that way she looks at me

Climbing up High, Climb up fast, I'm on my way to you, hear the sounds of the wedding bell chime, come on, Climbing up High, Climbing up fast, I'm Living on High for you. You're the One I know I love, you know it's true. Come on.

Flying through the clouds, Flying through the skies, Flying through the Blue, I see my better half and that is you, feeling so free, feeling so young,

feeling I want to be with you, I feel your love, I feel your kiss, you say you do, I love you, I love you, I love you.
    Love that way she looks at me

Climbing up high, Climbing up fast, I am on the way to you, Climbing up Fast I can't wait to hear your voice of you, Climb up high, Climbing up fast, I am on the journey to you, I am dreaming to fly in your arms tonight, Live out Loud, Live it out Fast, I am Living on High for You........

RIDING ON THE TRAIN
TO HELL

*P*assing through the Bayous of Louisiana, the spirits of the dead sing in
the graves, they be calling to living men, living in the days of sin, they
curse and mock those mindless fools, the voodoo witches, the voodoo kings,
they all laugh at me, cause I'm Riding on the Train to Hell.*

*Born to be a lost soul at 5 years old, drank whiskey with my grandpa knows,
stole from stores, took bubble gum and cigarettes and who else knows, shot
my first man at the age of 8, smoked the dope till it was very late, I am a
sinful man who has not lived by God's right hand, I am a outlaw wild cat
who loves to cause Hell and spit in a lawman's hat, I'm a old damned soul,
that why I going to the underworld below. That's why I'm riding on the
Train to Hell, Riding on the Train to Hell, Ha Ha Ha*

*The Devil's Reaper became my keeper, he locked my soul away, from down
in darkness to the depths below, the river of the dead traps me so, night-
mares and goblins and ghouls to behold, I am a lost soul and I am very old,*

going to burn in Hell below, my crimes are pure sin, that's why I'm going to the Devil's den.

Riding on the Train to Hell, makes me want to yell, what the hell is happening to me, my mind is gone, my soul destroyed, my wife is dead and so is my life. I don't know what I am going to do, I just want to cry and boo.

The time for judgment is very swift, I'm going to burn for causing a fit. I'm a lost soul that's why I'm Riding on the Train to Hell, Riding on the Train to Hell, I am riding on the Train to Hell!

SCREAM BANSHEE SCREAM

*S*ouls coming down, Skulls of Pain, Rage, Rage, Rage, The Women in white comes to me, Evil and Cruel, Deadly cold rising from the grave, Ghoulish sight to see, Scream Banshee Scream.

Come to me my darling bride of death, come to claim my dark soul today, Take me to the other side where the spirits dwell and reside, I can see the fire inside your heart tonight, You came back to life to take my sorrow for you,

I missed your dark call, but I am here to descend to the fall.

Mistress in white, I know your game, you're are my guardian of death in the eternal flame; I see the wheel of fate and is spinning bright, the cycle of death, life, rebirth bring me into the light. O you make me bleed, Scream Banshee Scream.

Time to go the other side of life, Death is but a door my dear, Heaven I must wait to see, until I go I must stay in Limbo's time. Passing through the spirit wells the sickness spreads through the way, sucking down lost soul's pain.

Sadness I can so see, the ones You lost were your family tree, how sad is the pain to see love ones gone this way, Bring up out of the grave, I have seen enough of the pain.

Rivers run red drenched in shame, Ten zillion souls killed by humanity's ways, I can't believe what evil is evil today. Mistress in White, tell me, tell me, please, why do you show me these things.

The Lord of Heaven cries in pain, Man is the fallen creation, damn the evildoers that seek to kill, let them burn and boil in the great flame called Hell.

Free me, now I am leaving, time to climb to Life, time to tell the tale of life. I have seen enough death to count too many lives, Now I am free.

Scream Banshee Scream.

THE ENEMY WITHIN

The Devil comes to tempt your soul
He knows your mind and He knows your goals
He does whatever it takes to give
You corruption and hate
Do what thou wilt is his
Law, who gives a Hell what religion
Says it's all bullshit in Lucifer's name
The Enemy Within

The Father of Lies makes sin
Seem so good and good be bad,
God is angry and mad
The Enemy Within is my pain
In bondage to sin is the Devil's
game.

Fight the Beast in Christ's good name
He died on the Cross for all to
Be saved, if you do not then you will
Burn, Evil is The Enemy Within

Die, Die, you Evil Beast, I pray to
God to give me strength, give me the
Power, give me the hour, give me hope to
Kill the Enemy Within

I just want to fall and fade
Into emptiness, let me die, let me bleed, fall in shame, God please save me,
Save ME

The Devil comes tempt your soul
He knows your mind and He knows your goals
He does whatever it takes to give
You corruption and hate
Do what thou wilt is his
Law, who gives a Hell what religion
Says it's all bullshit in Lucifer's name
The Enemy Within

I can't stand to see pain of sin
Around me, demons come to trap my
mind, Temptation feeds the evils I know,
How much longer will Heaven not hear
My cries,

I just want to fall and fade
Into emptiness, let me die, let me bleed, fall in shame, God please save me,
Save ME!

The Devil comes to tempt your soul
He knows your mind and He knows your goals
He does whatever it takes to give
You corruption and hate
Do what thou wilt is his
Law, who gives a Hell what religion
Says it's all bullshit in Lucifer's name
The Enemy Within

Rage, Lust, Fire, and Blood
Where is the Dark One
I hate you, you disease, God will kill
You demon beast, Die Die Die,
You murderer of the good.

I just want to fall and fade
Into emptiness, let me die, let me bleed, fall in shame, God please save me,
Save ME

The Devil comes tempt your soul
He knows your mind and He knows your goals
He does whatever it takes to give
You corruption and hate
Do what thou wilt is his
Law, who gives a Hell what religion
Says it's all bullshit in Lucifer's name

The Enemy Within

FREEDOM

What is Freedom?
Freedom is the power to change the worst circumstances into the best.
Freedom is Liberty.
Freedom is Happiness.
Freedom is Power.
Freedom is the right to have your dreams come true.
Hail O Holy Liberty! Set all people free!

LITTLE MISS WITCH—
PART DEUX

*H*ey Little Miss Witch you sexy cat, you put a love spell on me and
that's a fact. You got black magic and furry cats, fangs sharp as a
vampire bat's, fly this night across the moon, feel the freedom at hand from
the clergy robed man. Burning the witches did they burn, false hood they
claim so untrue. Who are they to judge any soul, how they ask for praise
from the people in the pews, yet they take your money for whores, drugs and
gold. False men of the cloth, just as corrupt as our hearts enthroned.

Hey Little Miss Witch you sexy cat, you put a love spell on me and that's a
fact. You got black magic and furry cats, fangs sharp as a vampire bats,
you love to tempt me with your succubus eyes, yet I don't care I will love you
for all time, yes I love you, between your hypnotic stare, the spell worked but
I loved you before you cast your work in the potion that you brew. You did
not know, how much I cared, I don't judge you who you are or what you do.
We were misfits when we were young, dear sweet friends, mistreated and
blamed, you protected me and I protected you, for this my heart is yours no

matter what you do. You may steal, kill, or destroy, but I don't care because for me you were always there. I was alone and you were there, a friend to talk to when no one cared. You cried in my arms and wept dear, your own family cast you out like a fallen angel too. So we were alone together, two desperate souls in love, but we made our own path, mystics and white witches, healers too. We fix broken hearts, we mend destitute souls, as long as we are together, what more could anyone want, so cast your spell on me I will cast mine on you, as long as we are together, that is all that matters.

Hey Little Miss Witch you sexy cat, you put a love spell on me and that's a fact. You got black magic and furry cats, fangs sharp as a vampire bats, let's make love for all life, never let me go, nor will I in return, since we were children we used to pretend and play, you kissed me, wearing your sisters black lipstick and I thought you were cute, you taught me the way of the craft, nature in respect of all spirit exist on this natural path. Magick of Hour! Magick Of Hour! Light your Black Flame of Love around my Dark Bride, loyal I am to her and she to me. For as long as love shall last, but I wish more for a life time will be. In Summerland I hope we shall be together, forever, you and me. Upon this day, Blessed Be.

DUALITY

Good and evil exist in us all. How far do men climb and how far will they fall.

I wonder so, what is the purpose of this mistaken duality, why do we struggle with such imperfection of soul, of wind, of life, of the earth and the trees.

Let us fly to lands beyond, ether or stars, to a paradise, some where there is bliss, peace, love and charm.

Why is there so much pain in the world, why is there not love and kindness in this horrible world.

I used to think that mankind could change, but more and more do I see greedy, selfish and cruelty.

When will it all end and man awake, his deep slumber, his mind too numb to care, maybe we need a second time to get it right, or maybe we should just continue to fight.

Killing and living, breathing and dying, why is the way the world the way it is?

We seek fortune, fame and glories beyond the norm, yet we cannot take it with us when our time is gone and done.

What will men take when they are dead? Some say there is no immortality, others say there is. But still what a wasted life if all you live for is pleasure.

Compassion and love, is the true purpose of life, Kindness and mercy is the way of the soul, man should learn, history repeats itself day and day out.

We turn on the News and see the same story every day, yet we would rather care about celebrities, money, sex and who knows what.

Is man that cold? Has his heart no desire to change or learn or grow, to become a better person is better to know. Status, Education or Class will not mean a thing when one is dead.

No one truly cares when the rich and famous are dead, they mourn them for awhile then they look for something else to think about, such stupidity.

If all that is what it is about, then the world would be better to return to the time of Cain.

What a sad waste, for the world that does not care. Delusion and Illusion is all people seek. To piss away life and all things.

THE HERO'S JOURNEY

M en, women and children are all on the journey of life.
We grow up and change, but change into what, some turn out bet-
ter than others in thought, sight, sound or touch.

What does inspire you? Do you know? If not, I say, please, learn study
and grow.

You were put on this earth for a Divine purpose. Whether you believe
it or not!

Fulfill your dreams and accomplish your goals, do not throw away the
talents and gifts you have been given inside our soul by God almighty.

You can do anything your heart desires, push forward and believe it,
and then you will achieve it.

Sometimes, sacrifices must be made, but it will pay off in the long run
if you do not quit. The journey is hard for all people with dreams: Writers,
Poets, Filmmakers, Painters, Musicians and yes even Politicians who seek
to create good change in the world today.

I tell you this dear friend; do not think you will lose by fate.

You make your own choices, both good and bad.

So be very careful in how you choose to live.

The future is not set, it is always changing, but you can decide the outcome by what choices you make in the present.

We are always in the present, until it becomes the past and tomorrow is the unknown future.

Be strong and have faith, work hard and work smart. Make connections and invest your money and time wisely. Learn everyday even if it's just for a few minutes, you might be surprised what you learn.

HOOKAH AND ABSINTHE

*W*hat love is this strange delirium, the devil's delight and the green fairy, they embrace in vivid hallucination. Erotic maybe, passionate definitely, when you taste that licorice sweetness upon thy lips it's great to bend down and kiss your young wife's loving breasts.

Making love when you are stoned, is quite fun then to bone.

But Absinthe and Hookah are not just for romance, no they are great to have after a good dinner with friends or family or anyone at best.

Tales of the Hookah have come far and wide. A love flavor filled smoke to fill my lungs sublime. Taste of peach or apples or mint such a lovely aroma it is.

And there is Absinthe; rare it is come by, a sad misunderstood drink that the law decrees is shy, propaganda that is really false like the ties of Reefer Madness which is hopeless to the fault.

So I say drink of that green scented liquid flame; it is better than wine and has a much nicer bouquet.

MARIJUANA QUEEN

S *moke and smoke, puff, puff and pass*
The green leaf of healing is good for what aliment is vast.
Natural in making, a pleasant sensation, rites and ritual be not needed.
A good medicine in treating discomfort and physical pain.

Legalities are in a manner of opinion. Men in political parties and re-ligious fanatics in pointy hats, declare that is the most dangerous substance on earth, yet I am sure that they have done it themselves in the past or not. I don't know nor should anyone care.

No for true reasons that have been suppressed, it has been outlawed by Government and corporate greed, let gangs and cartels flourish with drug dens indeed. Oh I forgot, it helps the underground economy.

No, I say, to the evil of corrupted Politicians! How dare you rob man of natural medicine!

It heals pain that synthetics do not help. It treats cancers that people are dying from. Do you have cancer or AIDS or a virus that cannot be cured? No, then go to Hell!

Who are you to decide what people should use to relieve them of their diseased aliment and sorrow?

It does not kill people it is natural, the way nature intended it to be.

Young and old are thrown into jails, for a victimless crime. It is not arson, or rape or murder or theft. No, it's just someone who wanted to ease their physical pain. Hell, Beer and Cigarettes are worse. They do kill the mind and body.

So support legalization, and let all lovers of ganja be set free.

IMAGINATION IS MAGIC

*B**y the power of the human spirit's mind, we see things in the darkness at night, in dreams we fly to other realms, worlds of wonder, bizarre or weird indeed.*

Imagination is more important than science, but science is still important.

The human soul and animal soul is of spirit and all spirits, human or not, dream at night and in the day.

Dreams manifest into reality, As Above so Below.

The spirit world is the land of dreams, dreams that give warning or premonition, prophecy and inspiration.

Paint your dreams and write them down, you may just have a great idea for something to invent, create, build, cook, bake and shake.

So many wonderful things were made by people who had fantastic dreams. Look at what splendors the world has because of innovation of mans imagination.

Animation, Video Games, Theme Parks, Stories, Inventions and improvements to medical science, space exploration, discovering wonders and buried treasures of life and fish and prehistoric creatures in the mysterious seas.

I say this, Imagination is Magic and without its endless possibilities, men and women would not survive, nor explore nor dare to learn new things.

Never underestimate the power of the human spirit, for God gave us the imagination to do amazing things. Use it for good and not for evil and you will find such things about yourself that you did not know were possible.

Yes indeed, Imagination is Magic.

THE PROPHET AND
SPIRITUAL JOURNEY

*T*he Prophet and the Seeker of Spiritual Knowledge are similar but not the same.

The Prophet is chosen by the Divine but also knows in his heart that it is his life's purpose to serve God.

Some people may think that is a drag. But for someone who loves God as a friend it is a blessing. God is not a killjoy although many people now days seem to think so.

But look to a higher understanding as I have in my seeking.

I have found that God is amazing and very kind and loving.

Like any divine parent he wants the best for all his kids and even those who are not his children.

The Prophet's job is to inspire people to come to God, but come freely of their own will. Men should not force religion down people's throats or use a selfish agenda for their own means.

God does not give a damn about organized religion or rituals, no he cares about your heart and to have a friendship with you. He is a gentleman of course and will leave you to your own decisions.

But how I wish people would come to God, many sadly don't want to know Him and even hate Him. Yet if they would seek knowledge and understanding from his view, as a Father tries to instruct his Son or Daughter, then they too could see things from a proper perspective and grow to become better people.

If one does seek to become a seeker of God, and you mean it. You will find him and he will easily find you. You will find peace in your life. I say this from experience. Look into your heart but above all look to God for advice in all matters, if he did not care he would not listen. And even if you don't think He is listening to your prayers, he does.

This was my case in my own life.

Some ask why does God let evil exist in the world, remember that we are at war with the powers of darkness, it does not matter if you believe it or not. Evil exists, that is just how things are. God does not want people to suffer, but he can use personal suffering to help a person blossom into a better person.

It's called building character, do this and you become a champion and grow a lot in life.

ART AND MUSIC

*A*rt and Music, so much culture, so much creation, the world has advanced so much because of it and has grown to inspire many, we have so many styles of music it is funny and not.

Classical is wonderful, what beauty and brightness is in hearing the great ones like Mozart, Brahms, Bach and many more.

Jazz is fire and dance and song, New Orleans and New York. Hot damn how smoking is Jazz.

Heavy Metal, a feast to the ears, the gods will shake and rumble for such a devious fun noise as Metal.

Reggae and Ska, Punk, New Age, Gospel and Gothic, They're all nothing but good times.

Listen to music and grow.

Art, Painting such great things and places and people have been caught by life to canvas. What would the world be without Da Vinci, or Van Gough or Pablo Picasso; we would be bored that is what. Learn the arts they are very pleasing to the soul and mind. Draw and Sketch, Draw and Sketch, Draw and Sketch.

VINCENT PRICE

*A*n interesting rogue indeed, a lovable yet sinister scoundrel and an enigmatic actor to root for, he was an awesome soul.

Such a fiend on the camera but a man I would love to have met and be friends with if he was still alive, yes an interesting fellow indeed.

He could play the hero and the villain; the world will never have such a talent so missed as him.

Rest in Peace Dear Vincent, for the world loves you still and always will.

COMIC BOOKS AND GRAPHIC NOVELS

*T*he world of comic books and graphic novels, what a fantastic limit to the imagination, just kidding there is no limit.

Modern Mythos has come of these lovely creations, we so many inspiring stories of heroes, anti heroes and villains.

So many interesting adaptations made into games and films, not including some of the best animated series on Television.

We have comic book conventions and cosplayers, geeks, freaks and lovely ladies in sexy outfits that you would yank out your eyeballs from your socket and howl at the moon with desire and even give them complements, dirty or just plain nice.

Such a phenomenon as that the pictorial medium has exploded but was here since the very first days of man when we had prehistoric art drawn on cave walls by our ancestors. They were story tellers just like us, although bit more crude it was still effective for the time.

Let this inspiring medium known as comics never fade away from those who love them.

SUICIDE

Don't do it. It's not worth it. Enough said.

THE WEDDING OF THE DEAD
A VERY SHORT STORY

*T*wo lovers met and fell in love, a young boy and girl in their twenties, gothic outcasts and social misfits, but happy enough. But their mortal union was not meant to be when a lunatic robbed them one night while on a date and killed the young man's lover, lost and broken he retreated in vice, longing for his sweetheart's return from the grave.

On All Hallows Eve, he went to the cemetery to place dead roses on her grave, he wept with tears of shame, for had failed to save her during the attack and had kept the wedding dress she had bought and the engagement ring that she had given him.

He knelt down by her grave and wept all night, demanding that heaven open up to give him justice, he prayed in anger and frustration but no angels came to help him.

Instead, a figure of darkness appeared before him, it was the specter of his former lover, she was angry that he was there and told him to go away, he begged her to forgive him but she did not, and told him again to leave her so that she could rest in peace.

But he told her that he would do anything to regain her love, yes even after death, he could not move on in his human life, so she asked him.

How much do you love me?

He responded

"With all my heart, I would die for you?"

She was surprised by his replay and now felt sorry for abusing him.

He meant her no harm; he only wanted to be by her side. Visiting her grave made him happy, for the memories of the two years they had spent in love had brought him great joy and to her also.

Now she felt sorry for him.

He asked her this time.

"Do you still love me, even though you are rotting and dead?"

This phantom of his former lover was a mutilated corpse but still very pretty.

She said in return.

"I did love you but you and I cannot be together, you are of the living, I no longer am, "

"Is there not a way, we can still be together?" he asked.

She thought for a moment.

"Yes there is a way, but it is the most horrible of ways," she said.

"How?" he asked.

"You have to kill yourself to be with me," said the spirit.

"I cannot," he said.

"Then please go home and forget about us, you will find someone again," she said sadly.

"I will but I could have one wish, we will you let me kiss you, I don't care what you are, I still love you. I really do," he said.

She was surprised. She was afraid that she would be wanted even after this state.

She jumped in his arms, spirit and all and tried to kiss him but she went right through him.

He tried to embrace her but the result was the same.

She was sad and so was he. He had found her again and they still loved each other but could not be with each other.

He apologized and said good bye, and then left the cemetery to go home to his parents' house three miles away up the road.

But on the road, in the darkness while walking he was hit and killed by a drunken driver, and his spirit left his mangled body under the car.

He frantically tried to find his way in the darkness, but could not. He did not even realize what had happened to him and then he saw it. His own bloody body, the drunk driver speeding off. He saw his own death and was speechless about it. Now he was dead, but he remembered what his former fiancé had said and rushed back to the cemetery to find her.

Before dawn his spirit floated back to the site of her grave, she was still there and weeping.

"Don't cry," he said. "I am here for you," said the young man.

She looked at the ground not knowing what had happened to him and said.

"Jerry, why did you come back? You're alive and I am dead," she said.

"Sarah, I am dead too," Jerry said.

Sarah looked up in shock and saw the bloody spirit of her former lover.

They were now both dead, but out of the tragedy they were reunited and could be together again.

He smiled genteelly and took her hand to help her up from sitting on her grave.

They walked among the graves and smiled at each other, more happy being dead than when they were alive. A light from heaven shown down on them and opened a pathway for them to go up, they followed up as they did their clothes and appearance changed to be clean, their spirits full restored and looking young again. Jerry saw his love have a wedding gown on her and she saw him dressed in a groom's suit.

The Angel of the Lord appeared to them, dressed a robe of light, she was beautiful and had pink angel wings of great length and height, her eyes sparkled like a rainbow in the sky.

"Who are you?" they asked her.

"I am Seraphina, the Angel of Marriage, The Lord has heard your request for help, and you have been given it, come home you too, for you will have the wedding you always wanted but better than you ever expect," said the lady angel.

"Thank you," said Jerry and so did Sarah, as the angel led them into the Kingdom of God, there, they would live the true life eternal, together, forever as husband and wife.

The End.

BILLIONAIRES AND
MOVIE STARS

*W*e obsess over the rich and famous, movie stars and rock stars,
they entertain and titillate us just the same, scandal and extrava-
gance, but why?

Because the PR firms and News Media Hounds make it so, we worship
them and give them praise, sometimes a little too much. But what are they
in the end? People just like us. They entertain us but that is what they are
supposed to do. It is their job.

Overrated and over paid, much respect should be instead given to the
Billionaires who are philanthropists, now it's not true that every movie
star does not also do kind deeds to help others, many do but sadly the world
of Entertainment has changed.

The days of old Hollywood are long since gone, a sense of class and style has
been lost. I feel sorry for this current age of entertainers, will they even be

remembered 50 years from now. I don't know but I hope they will, not for the wild life styles they lead but for what they accomplished in the films they worked, music they made or inspiration they gave. Such artists are to be respected and my respect I give them, for if they were not given such unique talents to give us, the average citizen some relief and escape from the toil of daily life, we would drop dead of sheer boredom.

THE SERIAL KILLER'S PRAYER

*U*nholy *demons of the hour, receive my invitation to madness, rape and kill, rob and thrill, blood, torture it is all the same to me.*

Slit their throats, let the blood flow, taste their flesh and eat their souls.

Bathe in rivers of corpses, mass festering graves and tombs, mummies, zombies, angels who weep tears of sweat.

I grab my knife to hunt cooked sweetly man flesh, roasted in ovens hotter than hell, I drink the fluid from their intestines to ease my pain, the pain of living, let death take me I want to die.

But I will never stop the killing until my hunger is satisfied.

Woe unto the wicked man, this I am but I switched my soul for the Son of Sam.

I kill for pleasure, I kill for fun, I kill for no reason, just boredom really, it helps me get the job done.

Electrocute me and burn my flesh, because the dead tastes nice when they're are cooked serene.

Eat a man's liver with roasted chestnuts, a side of stuffed pig's head cheese and a nice vintage merlot will add to the taste.

I am mad and quite insane, but then madness is in all things.

One day I will die, I hope the vigilant will kill, little old me.

Then I will haunt them to the end of time.

But I am bored of this mortal coil, bored of all. Life is so dead, when you choose to fall.

So kill me and let me sleep; a coffin of fine pine wood is good enough for me.
*   Let me be cradled in the river Styx, let me float forever and dream of the damned for I hate existing among my enemies, stupid mortal man.*

I am the Serial Killer, I light the torch of strife, I show no mercy, I show no concern to people, I love no one and no one loves me. So I will leave a mark on the world behind. Bullies and Dimwits should not exist. Bless the avenger who does the job that the law will not, cowards and bat shit is all they are.

Now poison of bitter herb, Belladonna do I drink, my body numb and feeling weak. Now I go into darkness, sleep forever in dreams of pain, Hell is in this life! It is just as bad as the next. Twice damned and twice remembered.

Long live the Blessed, the Damned and the Dead!

UNEMPLOYED

*U*nemployed and hating it.

They lied to us and took our jobs, damn the Government, the Lying Politicians, the Bankers and the Elitist Mobs.

We went to school and got degrees, now we are stuck in debt because of the System's Greed.

Do more than protest, it does not mean a thing.

Start a revolution, start World War III, Rebel!

We are the 99%

We were not born into the undeserving rich or Ivy League schools like the spoiled brats, who did not earn it. Trust fund idiots they are. They give a bad name to those who work for it.

We came from all walks of life, and we work hard to get by. We are filled with strength because we have to survive.

The spoiled rich may earn their money, but let them help their fellow man, some do and this is good, others don't and it is selfish.

Create jobs for the country, you rich if you care then we will buy your products and maybe just care about what you have to say.

Let there be no class system.

I wish there was true equality among man. But there is not.

We live in the wealthiest country in the world, or so they claim. Yet many people who work an honest job are starving and can barely pay the rent.

In this day, there is poor customer service and people do not care if they insult a person that is different.

They whine and bitch, whine and bitch.

Shut up and grow some balls!

Stand up for yourself and take pride in the work you do, even if you don't like it, be thankful you have a job too.

At least you have a home to sleep in, food on the table and a family to keep you safe.

Count your blessing as small as they may be or what you make.

LONELY

*S*ad and lonely are many people. We grow up and are expected to flourish.

Materialism they say will ease the pain of life.

Let's build a bigger house to fill it with more stuff, but in the end that is all it is. Just simply stuff.

Better for man to build loyal friendships with people he loves, for if all a person seeks is material wealth, he is not truly rich. No, his is alone and has no true friends, thus he is truly lonely.

LUPIN TENDENCIES

Full Moon Rising, bomb fire building; let the dance of the wolf begin.

Prepare to transform to hunt in the dark forest of pine; rip your skin off, blood, pus and salt, fur to grow, hell to raise, fangs sharp to shred succulent flesh of woman and man.

The wolf shall kill the sheep tonight; taste the pleasure of sex and death, the same in one sweep of fright.

All in good time, the humans shall die; the lycans shall rise to reclaim the night.

Wolves are in man, but the beast must be embraced, claws to sharpen and prey to taste.

The rite of passage is soon to begin, sin eaters beware for we will devour your soul, and we need no false salvation by the men from Rome.

Run free in the shadows; be the infinite power of your totem's call, embrace your inner animal and be one with nature and all things in awe.

GALLERY OF BLOOD

*I*n the halls of pain, in the house of set, the gallery of shadows I see the souls *of the dead, trapped in images of torture and divine, paintings of trapped desires, forbidden pleasures, sorrow, suicide and never ending broken hearts.*

In the Gallery of Blood.

Who were these people, they walked the earth just like us; they lived, breathed and died but for what?

Some are children who killed their parents; some were nuns who were trapped by priests; these poor souls weep for their sin was lechery; they did not believe in their faith; now they suffer for hypocrisy's sake.

Others were lost because they did not care; to them this purgatory or limbo was a better place.

Dream forever, without any haste

In the Gallery of Blood.

LIFE IS SHIT

*L*ife is shit. It's shit because the way the world is run.

Life is shit because there are not enough jobs.

Life is shit because of racism.

Life is shit because people are poor.

Life is shit because of disease.

Life is shit because people do not fight against the tyranny of the land.

Life is shit because people are too lazy to change themselves to improve.

Life is shit, because there is no love left in a world gone cold, and what little love there is will soon be replaced with stone.

Life is shit.

SPIDERS AND RATS

*I*n the web of the spider does the arachnid make his plans; he catches his prey and drinks deep of his insect victims' blood; he is clever, smart and full of genius.*

The rat too, is a powerful little creature; they use wit to gather food and attract luck in the Chinese zodiac.

What interesting pets do they make, much better than crows or doves who are a bore, or slaughter on an altar, which streams of red rum that run deep.

All yes, Spiders and Rats.

OF BONDAGE AND BLOOD

*F*etishes are pleasure to eye of the beholder, indulge, taste, whip with chains, tie them up, pour on candle wax and make it hurt.

Bondage and Blood, Blood play, drink deep of the sweet wine from thy veins, the blood is the life the scriptures say.

What is love and sex without a little pain, romantic, yes, kinky sure.

But add some spice and you will feel nice. In Bondage and Blood.

ALEISTER CROWLEY

To the Most Wickedest Man in the World, a Man Who Was Ahead of his time. A great poet, an adventurous mountain climber, a master chess player who could beat any high roller any day of the week, an interesting story teller and exalted Magus, sadly misunderstood who lived life on his own terms and died by them. We do not know why he chose to go on the journey he did, but he had a great story to tell of his life in the end.

He gained fame and infamy by his strange deeds, but inspired the Magickal Arts quite indeed.

Rockstars and Film Directors have marveled at his life story.

Rumors and allegation have been in much speculation.

Jack Parsons and Ron Hubbard were also among his friends.

It was even said that The Great Beast was the grandfather of George W. Bush.

Why he did what he did we will never know. Oh well, farewell the Master Therion in Immortal Flames, Adieu.

THE CRYPT

The Crypt is where I bury my dead, my children, my wives, my grand-mother to sleep forever.

Where souls sleep in bodies of comatose flesh, rotting 'til the end of the world comes, when the Lord of Might shall return and resurrect

Us all to immortal form. Sleep now and dream in death, die well and dream free in the Crypt.

THE WITCH GODDESS

*H*ecate, the Queen of Magic. Hecate, Queen of the Night, mother of devils and harlots.

Invoke her not, for she shall take your soul.

Pray to her not, for she shall take your head.

Seek her not or you will see pain. Black Magic to steal your essence away.

JOSEPH CAMPBELL— THE MASTER OF MYTHOS

*F*ollow Your Bliss. Follow Your Bliss, Follow Your Bliss such a man of wisdom was Campbell. He did not have an ideology or theology, but he saw the universal truths of the human condition and human experience in the world of mythology, spirituality, psychology and storytelling.*

He laid a foundation to the formula of Mythos that screenwriters, novelist and artisans of all mediums use today to convey the message of the Hero's Journey.

He was a maverick but an inspiring man. He was a teacher to George Lucas and many others and taught us that you will find happiness if you follow your bliss, your dreams and goals in life. Do that and you will be content.

THE ASTRAL COVEN

*A*stral Vampires, characters and dearest of friends, children and souls created from the mind of a man, thought forms into reality, miracles abound. The power of imagination can turn a fictional character into utmost spiritual reality and even unto physical reality. The Ancients saw this mystical truth. The imagination is the power of creation; create your tales to bring your friends to reality and they will be. You may not see them before your very eyes, but in the spirit realm and in the dreamscape they will reside.

WARRIORS

*P*rotectors, Guardians, Soldiers, honor these men and women who fight. Fight for freedom, fight for morals, human dignity, mercy, justice and peace. The warrior way is self denial and self sacrifice.

Honor them, love them and cherish them.

The End

ABOUT THE AUTHOR

About the Author: Born Dominic Rocky Daniels, in the city of Anaheim, California in 1984, he was raised in San Gabriel, CA. At a young age his passion has always been in films, animation, and storytelling. He is best known for his dark fantasy / vampire book series: _The Damascus Chronicles_ (Book 1) & _The Damascus Chronicles: Denizens of the Night (Book 2)_, which has won the _Amazon Editors Choice Award: Best Books of 2014._

Trained in fine art at the age of 10, he decided to go into the entertainment business and become a writer. He is a self-taught author and the electronic dance music arranger under his Nega Blast X music production brand. He has a Bachelor Degree of Science in Media Arts and Animation from The Art Institute of California-Los Angeles. In his spare time he reads graphic novels and studies movies, his favorite music is heavy metal.

www.ingramcontent.com/pod-product-compliance
Lightning Source LLC
Chambersburg PA
CBHW060508030426
42337CB00015B/1792